The Castalian Crave

A Collection of Poems

The Castalian Crave

A Collection of Poems

FLETCHER DEWOLF

ARPress
ILLUMINATING IDEAS
EMPOWERING VOICES

ARPress
45 Dan Road Suite 5
Canton, MA 02021

Hotline: 1(888) 821-0229
Fax: 1(508) 545-7580

Ordering Information:
Quantity sales. Special discounts are available on quantity purchases by corporations,associations, and others. For details, contact the publisher at the address above.

Printed in the United States of America.

ISBN-13:   Softcover   979-8-89389-175-1
                    eBook   979-8-89389-176-8

Library of Congress Control Number: 2024916229

When the words leave the lips
and reach the bottom like sunken ships
no one can their treasure find
like lost thoughts in our open mind
they will float back to the top
as their meaning will never stop...

TABLE OF CONTENTS

CASTALIAN CRAVE:
A COLLECTION OF POEMS

THE BAR CZAR

SPECIAL COLLECTION
Owl Wonder Who

The Fifth Wheel

Chapter One: The Subjective Claws
of the Empire's Composing Machine

Chapter Two: The Sly Test Thought

A Breathing Spell

Poetry Space

A Collection Of Poems

A Collection Of Poems

FORMATION

A Collection Of Poems

THE MIRROR KILLS

Castalian Crave:
A Collection of Poems

Evolution

In the water not so deep
Live small creatures in their retreat
The world outside they cannot see or understand
Belonging to a quotidian man
His eyes fall short and seldom see
A part of what he used to be.

In Love

These cold feet that walk in grave
Mistakes were made but not to save
Chilling winds that blow the towers
Leave the day without hours
Words that capture all the eyes
Have poets searched to find and try
Explain this life as pirates might
Save their thoughts and chests of gold
All the other sailors told.
The poem it's locked the cabin door
Where I've sat and wrote before
No, my mind I cannot see
It's escaped the best of me
Once I had the light of day
All the space it's taken 'way
Over heads and borrowed time
I have looked but cannot find
Lost the arrow from my bow
It's in your heart—
Now I know.

After the World Began

If I were dead inside my tomb
I'd want to have some extra room
Where I could fly into the night
And spook some folks who did not right
To watch their hearts take an extra beat
That would be my evening treat
They'd never know I was in the room
Protected from my empty tomb
To see their thoughts so small and dull
I'd kick around inside their skull
With each terror I'd leave a lie
For them to live and never die.

Intoxicated Dualism

Books of battle written war
Yards of death combatant saw
Financed by the fools of fate
Driven by the date of hate
Hooked on holding hell a host
They've never put it past its post
Cries that crawl and create cramp
The light they've lost
And thrown out lamp
Bullets bit beyond their blast
Rods of risk they will cast.

Another Look

When sun sets low and people die
A song of death the caller sings
To birds who fly above the world and its hollow things
What words there are to make us think
Are often simple verse that lead us
    to that one last thought
That things could be much worse.

Treenail

The windows moving all outside
that it sees it cannot hide
wind it knows of its game
the arms of trees holds the music's breeze
when the walls talk to you
they know you will see through
beyond the forest and its cover
waiting for just another
lost and wondering without path
even they will have their wrath.

Paragraph of Pain

When the words wind around your brain
echo chambers where you find pain
let them go and make a line
with an end you cannot find
let them ask or let them say
just let them have their own way.

Put It Down

Stomach turns looks for knot
eyes blink the sun's too hot
they find sleep but dreams have got
twisted towards the point of sound
colors lead them all around
back to summer the music fair
floating landing in your hair
comb it out play each note.
that no one thought or even wrote.

Flat Head

We're not running in a race
there's no one we can't face
we've had speed beyond the light
played with pagans at their game
even though mine's not the same
had the devil in my house at night
as he left he spoke of fright
now you know who I am
just a person maybe a man
on a ride that never ends
holding on to so few friends.

Ride On

The summer shines in your eyes
bring the lakes their own surprise
chain and spokes with all those folks
sitting round the fire they're burning
let us know when you stop learning.

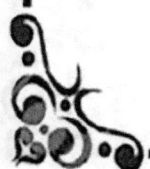

Distress

Troubles rise in smoke and flame
always coming back again
put them to the river deep
washed into the sea to keep.

Suppress

Feeling best when I am with you
knowing all that you can do
calling to the heart's desire
never smother or put out fire
if it burns the world to soil
never will our love then spoil.

Concluded

Complete thoughts have gone away
thinking that they are thought to stay
little simple how they be
belonging to the you and me.

Palm Reader

Follow lines inside your hand
life and death they say has plan
neither one I think is real
only what we're told to feel
as one day the world will see
what it meant it's supposed to be.

Old Line

Devil waits to call your name
you know by now that's his game
take you down to pits of flame
silly stupid little game
take you up to life unknown
as you were born you were shown
newest things they do grow old
like the stories you've been told.

Assertion

If your thoughts are incomplete
think them back and then repeat
wear them out if they persist
but when they come don't resist
they're only part of what you'll find
stored inside your mural mind.

Innovation

I see the wrinkles form on face
how the smoothness they will replace
you see the looks that slip from eyes
as if they had their first surprise
we know the start of better things
as the ending always sings
death has come today to be
more a part of you and me.

Checkmate

Double trance your deep inside
telling on the bishop's pride
played on angle sliding through
taking queen moved by you.

Benevolent

My mind has gone beyond its spell
wishing all to rest as well
warlock that I am tonight
has no reason left to fight.

Catch-All

The towel is full of old mildew
like lots of things that we all do
caught up in the blades of grass
watching sun make it pass
the road is worn with people's feet
now they call it an old street
the light is dim with night and dark
leading toward the base of park
sliding through the hours of fun
catching up with everyone.

Hidden

Buried deep inside your eyes
little truths with little lies
tears will wash them both away
so no one will have to say
of the past the present now
explaining why, when, or how.

Uncertain

Tear old pages from your heart
so you may make another start
build new mornings at your wake
so you won't have to stop and take
all the pain life's giving out
never knowing, caught in doubt.

Coated

Picture you with a thousand words
tending to the flocks and herds
sheep and cattle we do not say
act the same in our way
coats are made of their hide
put ourselves so deep inside
without them to cover us
we would act the same as if we must.

Begin

Put a flame to all your hate
bum it up inside your fate
give out love it doesn't hurt
even though you feel it might
once you do it's all right.

Explain

There's so few who ever care
what the world might wish to share
illusion wants you to see
time it gives history
palace has the gold in sight
days in love with every night.

Pages

Books were made to lose your mind
smoke with fire you'll always find
words are just another thing
that all people have to bring
to the point they wish to make
or the thought they wish to take.

Earth

Simple is the world so how
complicated it is now
mixed up like the leaves of fall
can we ever see it all?

Again

Work each day to beat the hour
life is spent in one's tower
looking down or seeing high
no matter how hard one may try
life will pass all of us by.

Simple Sister

When your words come out edgewise
    standing on their end
is it you or is it them who's trying to pretend?
either one as you decide
there is little that can hide
plain as day most things are
always near and not too far.

Your Head

There are things that are always there
that you won't see
no matter how long you stare
trails around the clouds
people hiding in the crowds
little meanings meant to hide
usually you'll find them deep inside.

Much

Love is lost and love is found
Love is silent and has sound
Love is long and love is short
Depending on how much you've got
Love can leave late at night
Or love can stay right in sight.

Relative Heathen

Towers with dust and candle lights
staring down on foggy nights
Christian pagans at their mass
praying for their prayer to pass
forgive the sins of their brother
only that they have no other.

Will-o'-the-Wisp

Pick your pencil, pen, or quill
sit and write your empty will
fill it out with much and most
read to those who you feel close
give the jewels you think you've had
to those pretending that they're sad.

Tell William

Off the head of your own son
split the apple and you'll be done
sentencing has just begun
as the nerve bends the bow
who will tell the arrow where to go?

Struck Measure

Out the wicket watches wonder
as the timber thinks of thunder
sleeping little dreams were made
underneath the tree of shade
when the fruit landed ground
the sleeper woke from its sound
while this verse makes you space
lightning strikes another place.

Bookish

Now you leave your simple mind
in the dust so far behind
learn with me the ways of old
that no other has ever told
pass the point of common man
common folks and drifting sand
desert of your mind explore
till you read a little more.

Suffering

Aches and pains they follow me
into worlds that I can't see
only feel to know they're there
or is it think to compare
which are words that show their bold
only throes who speak were told.

Assassin

Over to the end of time
runs the words we cannot find
thuggee lives on a street near town
no one prays he passes round
eyes are kept to see him come
hoping they are not the one
for him to take and then be done.

Undecided

Diamond dust or gold
just a few ideas were told
among those who thought they could say
what it is each day
that makes the world new or is it old?
neither one of the two really told
if it was bought or sold
it just would not come through
for conclusions that were true.

Talk Talk

Why the moon has talked to you and
 the sun stared you in the eye
as the trees held hands against the
 wind within the open sky
the road lead on to nowhere at least the sign had read
none of this was happening except inside your head
so all that is real to you or someday might exist
is completely dependent upon your
 own perception's twist.

History of Thought

Multitudes of speculation throughout the time of dawn
drawn tight by the shoestring of some forgotten son
holding close the followers of poetic verse and tale
the legends of all yesterdays stay lost inside to fail
scaling cliffs of conclusion about the world and such
and all its latent treasures that lie beyond our touch
the rhythms of the powerful and lost words of the weak
live inside this moment so to the next they might speak.

With Reality

There are no words that the pen can tell
    hidden deep within its well
there's no meaning that the bull won't hide
Troubadour, your wind will blow all the notes
the truth will know.

Intratomic

Energy inside of you waiting to explode
controlled by the reading of your secret code
voices from the sculpture calling in the den
where you left your paper, your pencil, and your pen
imagine that you're writing now that you've read
all the words the sculpture missed as it had said
see you sleeping half-awake to what I have to say
see the carving of the world has to give away.

Pendragon

Penates in your household, their pensile lead to others
Tom Thumb displayed by Barnum
they illumine the hearts as gin
imminence immensity on the PT circus
    ground inside the tent
the three rings ride imbroglio
time to imagine the inspired show.

Enchantnient's Entrance

Time made its first trick
as you disguised your rhetoric
the wax obscured the candle wick
as we were made to count above each brick
amaze the glaze between each piece
that lies inside observe the crease
and let all spells about this earth
rest upon their first birth
so we may not yet unweave
what others might have us believe.

Valhalla

Where goes the wind when it does not blow
how long is life before we know
who moves the world we cannot see
then recreates our reality?
some natural force or energy
made to last till eternity
or accidents performed by choice
the answers lie in the echo's voice.

Matinee

The world wrinkles, folds, and remolds
laughs at the movies
popcorn on its lips then discreetly slips to the next day
holding the observers in its prey
it bites hard trying to capture
its own real essence
removed from limelight in a midsummer's night
Shakespeare, what a dear, just pure literature
to fill the eye
with the graphic spy.

Trinity in the Garden

Evolution, fate, and luck
three words to which were stuck
wound inside a globe of taste
with little time left to waste
the clock ticks past the hour of dead
you remember what the gardener said
the day the flowers died
how truly hard he must have tried
setting out the young to live
and their death you could not forgive
evolution, fate, and luck
three words the flowers had forgot.

Dreaming Inside Yesterday

Your lips have miracles
on them you speak them off
they round the corner wearing glasses
with no eyes and a hat with no head
you'll remember every word they said
spoken with vulgarity
their meanings became more clear to see
the sky has had its eye wiped clean
no compassion has it seen
only age has worn its face
moving the clouds into place.

Undiscovered Thoughts

You've got the power
who measures it, we cannot see
yes, it comes for free
it's not involved with countless money
our minds are set to think this way
like a clock, they always say
when will they unwind
and go behind
to miss the starting hour?
their beauty peaks as a flower
we're lost in an ivory tower
stumbling on our psychic power.

Fading Drops

Days eroded empty into a cup
drank by a lonesome tulip drunk
in the garden growing toward the sun
the stars wait to watch it sleep
the flower has this life's beauty to hold and keep
the garden grows itself will fade
often playing with the shade
the rain has come, it will fall
without a reason, none at all.

Hobo

Twisted on a sidewalk headed toward the town
moving with the changes all above the ground
circus tents with novelty inside waits a clown
tickets to the performance
the wind blows them round
customers fill the side row
one soul walks the wire
'nother swallows fire
acts and events fill the day
the wanderer moves on his way.

Reincarnation

Two times the world has seen
three times woken from a dream
four times sat and wondered why
five times known and not replied
six times had a day then none
seven times lost then won
eight times moved without a chance
nine times filled with circumstance
ten times ten a life could be
one time real for you and me.

Repeating

Your brain grows cold inside its skull
the eyes of others have seen it well
what thoughts it has then will speak
are only those of the incomplete
now persons come and fade at last
so others might complete their pass
at life and times that seldom tell
that their eyes have seen it once as well.

Reluctant

The days grown old
the tide wipes clean
all childhood efforts
to become a dream.

Living Twice

To fall inside tombs of dust
then see beyond those colored dreams
how did you resolve all those schemes?
witted wonder inside paradise
thinking you lived this life twice
the wives of glory had you hypnotized
you never once became surprised
a way-off look had filled your eyes
amounts of wonder stayed till when
you began your life again.

War Wages in the Third Sense

How fine the superior minds have made
life obscure with plants of shade
the world will grow as tomorrow's war moves on slow
towards the technical engineer who lives so weak
with a strong fear he's had his thoughts
more potent in the school
the developed science of a fool.

Complacent

When your words are filled with spite
let them hide in the night
leave them far from your mouth
Civil War, see the South
blue and gray either way
it was all in yesterday.

Why

Coherent with riddles from the mountain peak
told all along the springs that run from
    near the top of hills who speak
green growing
buzzing with a laborious hum
I've yet known to be more than fantasy
where you will always leave me.

The Cascades

Cascading smoothed-out rock
small pools alone have turned their lock
camera of my mind has film
the pool is green and filled with light
sun it makes the most seem right.

Television Hepatitis

Strong quick movements to Hollywood's staircase
all downtown city-bound with imagination in the race
about the matter-of-fact no players yet did arrive
to make the show come alive
so was the curtain up or down
with the staircase on the edge of town
no one gave a shit
till the daily operas began when all would sit
in a mystified mongoloid condition
unconscious of their rendition
to the awesome routine
of being part of the scene.

Otherwise

You see the world through other's eyes
noticed looks that have surprise
held thoughts with hands so clean
never knowing what they mean.

Clever

When they indubitably give you advise
    that you've lost your mind
you can flourish in the foothills of adventures yet to find
there are the small dwarfs running through stardust
driving stagecoaches, selling rides, feeling that they must
to Kashmir, Trinidad, or Spain
but too much travel will lead you all the same
to theoplastic icons held inside the eye
watch as the worn-out road slowly passes by.

Part Two

They've graded off the lines of time
spelled them different so none could find
hidden mystery knocks on door
saying that there will be more.

Mind Service

How deep is your reality and will you intuit it?
is your life as long as death will sit or
    both the same unmeasurable?
how sharp the edge of explanation, playing
    tricks on the imagination
we talk to ourselves about the interior wall
that collapses into dreams at the end of each call.

Kaleidoscope Lineation

Writing the line of words with no road to ride
where the meaning sits and waits, wishing it could hide.

Behavior

Above the words the definition
who are you about to condition
you may have your position
but always mind the word magician.

Penological Devastation

Ardent practitioner mingling in the mind
levitation slides down, escaping the silent line
of the backsword beyond the perils inside
the tanistry of alliteration holding his head
    above the flight of passerine starlings
the clouds performed as cobblestones
the star chamber transliterated his actions
and added his photograph to the Rogues' Gallery
their earthly proceedings affected him none
their touchstone had no reputation of magnanimity
their malevolent revelations censured their own existence.

Treatise

Physical grace and perfection
just a small reflection
to controller of the void
the unthought thought unspoken word
one that ears have never heard
responsibility for every laugh
and tear all matter, mind, and mass
has its meaning that will pass.

Parallelism

First page of compassion torn out from the book
second page makes another look
third page floats in an illiterate sea
fourth page never reached the eye
fifth page slowly began to die
sixth page never answered why
seventh page closest to the end told of an
    extreme state when
the eighth page advised you to read it again.

The Raven

Contemplating the crevices in the concrete
    while assuming the altitude of the
    butterfly and its perfection
the raven evaded obtrusive observers, its
    flight stung the skylarks skill
of skeleton smokestack landings and
    cast aside the credibility
of Einstein's theory
that velocity determined its form
an independent pilot inside the realm of exultation
soaring to the heights of genetical, geological genius
resting in the nest of notability.

If You Let Them

You design this interior that soothes your mind
and welcomes your thoughts and if it turns to sand
you can make it a castle for you to live in
with a drawbridge so no one can get in
unless they swim the river
of your mind and sneak inside to burglarize your eyes
and take your emotions to dinner while
    dieting on your feelings
they might invade your physical form and gasses
    and become your last idea or fantasy
if you let them float downstream to the pool of your entity
your deepest secret self down there
    at the bottom of the well
if you let them.

Purview

Clean the paws of curious cat
rolling, wondering on its back
birds they know her claws see sharp
through their feathers and the dark.

By Yourself

When words start to stare you down
look you up and all around
see what you hide is not so deep
give out secrets that you keep
take you over then back again
with control of your pen
physical and abstract too
think who made these words for you.

Deaf

As the words drip and dance
thinking that they have a chance
to perform within their ear
seeing what they cannot hear.

Woven

If night was night for rest and dream
those who play have not yet seen
serious this game of sleep
with each day it has you keep
going back to where you've been
in a dream that will not end.

Answerably

Above the sea sky and air
who writes the rules that we care
is it man, ghost, or God
they've cut the answer with a sword
cloud as pillow sky as bed
sun has told us words ahead
of the dream we call space
in the air there is a place
to rest the thought that holds you down
flying past the speed of sound
thinking of the truth so high
wonder why it passes by?

Beguile

After winds have stopped to blow
leaving sand where it would go
silence makes its final speech
to see how far it may reach
talking to the still of night
even if their long and drawn
out they go before the dawn.

Compounded

From the eye there runs a tear
in the heart that had no fear
knowing that the mind had said
it was behind and not ahead
so it was inside a sphere
where it could not make things so clear.

Observe

The cat has seen the light go out with the doubt
now you know this trick I play with a secret
that won't say how it's done
I have your will inside of me to keep still.

Clandestine

Over past the point of now
we have left the reason how
holding to the final day
when we give our secret way.

Necromancer

Magic is my game of chance
so we play with romance
to the point that it will end
as the birch was made to bend
back to sky the ice has gone
on the branch of you too long.

Indian Summer

Outside of doors that have no hinge
walk the steps on the fringe
to the garden where you meet
flowers give their place complete
growing as the path you cover
makes you see yet another
way to look at things outside
knowing that you've always tried.

Skulduggery

The wind has blown beneath your door
and brought the cold with its core
how the dramas with magic spin
with white wings they laugh and grin
no sound has made their ears turn in
to where the dream will begin.

Simple Remedy

How your mind works or does it play!
you might be the one to say
the miracles make it whichever way
the simple have the most to say
unrecorded in a forgotten way.

Some Gruesome See

Chewing on skulls and diminished brains
the blood runs dry inside their veins
students of the graveyard
scholars of the night
calculating curiosity until their final bite
death rides inside a boxcar
moving slowly beneath the North Star.
the world has come to rest and be
calling to the moon above the sea
it asks why you wait for me.

Landmark of the Intellect

You wanted to be inspired and stimulated
articulate and educated
surprised at no invention
never having to pay attention
rooted in the wisdom of Socrates
with parables that were sure to please
never asking when or why
the first bird began to fly
until you fell out of the nest
landing among all of the rest.

Over Again

Smothered in rays of light that no one saw
removed from reach the candle stares
the walls fold then teach the eyes
to follow words that wrap into poetry
spoken from a distant balcony
the time it has none
the people they stare and turn
astonished with approaching auras they always learn.

Marionette

The synthetic symphony romantically moves
        beneath the closed doors
floating on top of marble floors
hollow of risible tone
the fools understand themselves are alone
inside a puppet life set on the stage
without a knife to cut their strings
complicated by the musical things.

You and Fantasy

Life unfolds in sunsets of mystery
death sits inside
black stone we carve with sharp spells
that cover the imperative walls
which cast shadows
of our fantasy role.

Picaresque

Shoals of drolls where myrtle grows
as power falls and folds
wager not the thunder
the birth of any new sight between assertion not lightly
matched you have your clever delight.

Tartarean Truth

Exactly why the words were made
to filter the grade
or who the word-creator might be
never seems to interest
the observer's test
or any of the rest
who generalize through the wizard's eyes.

Uncommon Sense

People come to eternal surprise
where the thought lies
and you're waiting for the news
with worn-out logical shoes
that explain the day is night
and all is right.

The Same

Suspended in the height of stupidity, the last frontier
once intelligence notably acquired itself
a fluke in the presence of plagiarized ideas
that mold and ferment in the cellars of
    some nervous tissue
above the neck of knowledge.

Attraction with Fraction

Like a stomach you grow full
of the words that start to pull
your attention is not so great
till you have known your fate
I could sit and read your palm
or some other bible psalm
whichever one interests you
of them both I've read a few
honest in my magic game
like no other plays the same.

Grave Decision

Sepulchre of the wicked holding out its arms
whet your physical priggish prima donna
      who moves the night
your eye, ear, and sight.

Difficult Decision

When the sweat pours like rain
you'll really know it's work again
who designed this world to turn
with many minds that never learn?

Proportionality

Reading writing worn-out pen
spelling words once again
over hills of meaning came
walking old man with a cane
pointing towards the lake of doubt
with his stick he pointed out
errors in the sky were made
covered by the clouds of shade
perfect is this sun that shines
reflecting of the lake then pines
taking dark from the earth
giving life its total worth.

Present Present

Kill the past and bury deep
or it will have you often weep
though the future has its spell
now is better just as well.

Open Sesame

If you have read my open mind
tell yourself what you could find
in the depths of love and hate
arrive most people much too late
to see the game of opposite
is nothing more than what you get.

Vault

Put to work the mind of power
crowding thoughts within the hour
put to rest your horse of pain
along with love you've had in vain
give yourself one last chance
to follow words that often dance.

Yet

Over through your mind rides love
in your heart held with a glove
lives your last desire
don't light that match, it's on fire.

Just Then

When you think all is clear
simple, little, plain
you'd better have another look
and see nothing is the same
when you know that you have made
your last turnabout in life
watch the wizards carve the world
with their wishful knife.

Interlacing Words

Wearing carpets made for magic trail
in the sky where they can sail
landing in the tapestry town
where no chance could there be found
asking author with his pen
if he would ride and write again
speaking with their woven mind
hoping he could once unwind
all the spells that come with verse
making trails to fly less worse.

Rossum's Universal Robots

Magnets pull your metal hand
up toward head to understand
beauty turns your eye toward it
as you know both will sit
in a secret frame of mind
builds the reflection one won't find
without the key that fits the lock
to the door you'll never knock.

Hypnotic Pleasure

Point-blank point of view
pointing toward the pointless few
on a scale of one to two
present passed the words who knew
to the others in their mind
looking for a different line
hypertension set at ease
written so the sound would please.

Driftwood

When your brain has paid its tax
thinking that you will relax
on comes looking devise with eyes
dreaming as it is surprised
drifting toward its final rise
with the mind that's little wise
that has a know it never ties.

Phlegmatic

If time stands in your way
counting slowly every day
turns its page apathetic
towards yourself it won't be clear
hiding swiftness with dispatch
leaving haste that you can't catch.

Time of Man

Transplanted into the spheres of sight that move to
    transparent mountains set to unwind carefully
refashioned for foolishness men playing powerfully
skys open to them
with stairways that have scrupulous
    steps that they fall upon.

Rote

Defining and unveiling the wounds of society
can catch you in fallible fisheries with romantic mysteries.

Brain Factory

The illusion of paper and words can always grow to more
than how they seemed to be
yesterday blowing past your door
lightly in the wind
now the words are heavy and won't let you begin.

Catenated Cosmologies

Tour de force and entourage
how the words become so large
the voyeur sees his unusual sight
the courtesan stays overnight
these riddles wind the clock too tight
the clairvoyant leaves the atmosphere
as the mathematical atrophies begin to appear
emulating felicities of fallout shelters clear
as the underground is filled with fear.

Archfiend of Verse Architecture

The old town crumbles
new waves arrive on the shore
dauntless daughters in dreamland
reaching out for more
the epic erodes their deaf mute minds
they are now not so finical
as one begins then sees
so the lines might please
if they could touch them, even speak them through
and hear them chime inside of you.

Validating Vanishment

When your writer becomes a ghost in your own graveyard
but no matter where you look, finding him is hard
all of life has held you down to its secret stone
do you think the author is buried here alone?

The Poetaster

Most pithy trick of surveillance
semantical verbosity
got your transcending character
reflecting images of society.

Chamber

When the floor touches ceiling
leaving walls without no feeling
in the room you used to be
and once found so appealing
out of space it speaks to you
telling how its life is through.

Seeking Searcher

You've always had to interpret
situations through your heart and not your mind
or you would have never been
left so far behind.

Explore

In the closet of crafty criticism reassuring
    the dramatist the act is obsolete
the artist that the frame has faded broken by the feet
buried in the depths of perception
this has become our moment of reflection.

Music of Mankind

You've seen the people fall, seen them crawl
with no use of it all
you've wondered why the rain feeds the sea
are the flowers in style?
does the earth's face smile?
how long has man had this life?
how many tomorrows will he be?
how many yesterdays was he?

Lost Arts

Even though it's a thing they've never seen
most art begins inside a dream
and the secrets to our mental maze
drift slowly into yesterdays.

Castle of Necromancy

The drawbridge closes
its secret and cold inside the walls
it was said there is a witch who calls a rare list of names
to gather in the courtyard for first-hour details
to where the spells do lie and how a distant
    look fills every eye
with expectation till the fog settles
out beyond the bridge to surround the field and flower
never forgetting
their first cold secret hour.

Lunar Highlights in the Headlines

Terrorist on the edge of town
with the graveyards burning down
motion of the production line
making up this life
the doctor calls his patient closer as a
    wife conversations held before
spoken in a tower shivering down its
    steps out through the hour
may you have this dance upon this narrow line
the net we need not below us this time
so balanced while we're asleep
then we wake up dreaming
watcher of the world
we are redeeming

Orchestra of Ornaments

Sun burns the earth to crust, rivers run to sea
that rest in the beds beneath their cosmology
you asked the forest for reasons
and the trees all stood apart
separate from their roots, pounding in their heart
the oneness was no contract, no doctrine read their wills
the power of the wind blew scenes
while rushing down the hills
floods of words have you wondering
pretentious of their ends
the rules read the measurements, counting all your friends
reflecting their images that never seem to last
the mirror says it has grown tired of past.

Drift Age

Fireside secret lift in rhyme
to be told another time
words that made the ear bend near
so rare and hidden one could not hear.

Drifty Drumbling Writer

Sits up to the page of power
it outlines him by the hour
points to toil and wish command
the captured verse he'll understand.

Memory

Smithers, flinders, smock, frock will fly off the workers
as they try to hold the long shirt in its place
the wind will take it without a trace.

Plan It

Life with death and power of things
are only words the world still sings
said to it in days of past
it knows itself will always last
beyond the heart and mind of man
that's buried deep below the sand.

A Dualistic Mind

When I see the design of your thought
I remember the memories that you forgot
holding on to the flower of spring
we both will remember everything.

Native Soil

The breeze of verse will blow through your leaves
as your roots grow over me
like the earth 1 become to be.

Owlet Too

Wipe the dust off the poetic screen
that keeps you watching in a dream
clean the webs from a sleeping owl's eye
that watches night and will not cry
sitting in a spruced-up tower
who will arrive upon each hour.

Yearning

Words can move a mind toward age
turning slowly every page
or bring it to a day of youth
with pains that leave with wisdom's tooth.

Without the Cloud Seeding

Way into the day that cries
comes the night with rainy eyes
past the point of no surprise
with the wind the fog floats then flies.

Invisible Caster of Lots

Playing card tricks without a deck
music without a sound
all good hands have been laid down
a bet is made for the whole town
a leader of the sorority makes a point the cards can see
dealer of the deck unseen
sails tonight in his first dream.

Chapter One

In a New York Second

Raw skull with gray mind matter
served upon a silver platter
made to speak then start to chatter
it stares you down to jaws that shatter
leaving dust and teeth that tatter.

The Actor's Diary

Few that have a mind of verse
that they may speak and not rehearse
for many who will act out play
give their lines and roles away.

Wrath of Grape

Tales of truth will never tell
who drinks to bottom of the well
secret swallow made its last drop
a taste of wine that would not stop.

Send-off

The music turns to a dark passion glide
where worries leave and take a ride
on notes that were written to end
in brief explanation of why they should send.

A Marline Spike

Murder on the high sea
marline spike in heart of captain
will not come free
crew is roaring without their oar
sail is blowing toward different shore.

The Act of Casting

Murky fog patch sets on mind
pillars crumble with the time
witch swallows up the broth of night
casting spell that's out of sight.

The Badminton Teamster

The shuttlecock lightly hit her in the eye
only a small tear came for her to dry.

Glover Knows the Rule

Pointing hand with fingers crossed
which direction now is lost
glove that's never met the cold
waits for thumb that has it sold.

Nightcap

Dust of barn has seen cow sleep
as it waits for webs to keep
angles made design is trap
for fly to land and slowly wrap
its wings in snares
that won't let flight
have its way from wrack of night.

Exotic Birds in the Jungle of Ju Ju

With tricks upon their colored wings
charming air to slide by all feathered things
near in the sky.

Barmaid Learns Board Rule

When days are made of silver
and knights ride for gold once more
again the billet will fold where measured
acts are played for jest
and joints watch beneath the rest
to hear what is best.

Jackanapes

Nimble, quick, wax with wick
burns for one who waits to pick
height of flame and burning stick
is only what they have to lick.

Unblamable Slaying

As hounds come home
the gray fox runs now alone
horse is tired
sleeps in stable
and dreams of dogs
that were not able.

Witch of the Two Will Spell

Wet cat crawls from lake with cry
burlap wrapped on claw not dry
shaking off the drops of death
walking now more sure of breath
prowling instinct recalls man
holding rope that tied with hand
a knot of deadly desire
inside a swallowtail coat she thought
there is no heart of fire to note.

A Fitchew at Sea Level

The king's evil about your neck
the words were written upon a deck
of ground, wave, sea
surface of the earth and tree.

Fire Raid of the Knowledge Bin

Warlock on the top of word
speaking but was never heard
the notes of air will wait
for wind to blow them to the watchful eye
that reads its lust
will blink upon this note of dust.

Panic Charm

Cast a cloth upon your head
a tapestry of poetry lead
past the fields where a Jack in Pulpit stands to care
for the forest beauty fare.

Preindicate the Virus of Stupidity

Mantis weaves a web they cannot see
this line we read is dark and clear
as the objective reality has come near.

The Digester

The roses grow over door, stonework, mortar, more
bench it holds the squire of wonder
past the castle he will ponder
all the travels with their thunder.

Over High

Overrun, wilted flowers next to grave
beat by showers
see the day as soul would say
observes the beauty pass away.

Fulgent Frequentation

Frere will travel often far
on seashore drive where others rode
to survive the journey's story as told
without a notice that it is old.

Outside the Range of Intellect

Alluding to the secret power
that makes life proceed inside a marble tower
a drawbridge lowered each fourth hour
six a day to other side
where transcendent tales have left to hide.

Out and Out

Wind blew clear through foggy night
the stager acting on stage of life
has long ago begun his act
with experience it grows more exact and old
as one actor saw a player told.

The Propounder

Lightning hits the rod on barn
striking out its first alarm
the hay is dry and will burn fast
as how he wishes his thoughts would last.

Fully Realized

Who will rule and have it done
where the world has sat and spun
round the lives of people small
looking for the sense of all.

Rhodochrosite

Where the sound hides in crack of floor
starts the story of few feet, if more
who walk the plank to meet the sea
that holds the shore beneath its plea.

Great Circle Sailing

Shallow person through the window stare
lost deep inside the view out there
feeling that the sea is near though the deck
was washed so clear
with all the sailor's sunken fear.

Fulminating Power

Arab wants the lateen sail with a long yard
slung toward the mast
the weaver has woven cloth so tight
the wind will ask who holds it in its flight.

The Jeu de Mots Threshold

Pick the time the ink will spill
the clock will read high noon until
the door of sayings swings both ways
inside as hinges act in plays.

Saloon Car

Sedan driving toward the shop
where spirits are sold and left to drop
the image of the fancy fair
has clouded over deep despair.

Pronunciamento

Compass card in deck of galley
thirty-two points toward Sally
jeu de mots will answer slow
overboard the proof sheet will go.

Bouquet of Stone Crop Watching

Smoke jack in the chimney gas
on wheel will turn the spit
till winds finds its breeze to fit
character of the wood crusade
stood next door being made
chiseled from the granite stone
he watched the smoke rise alone.

Braggadoccia

The words of watchful eye will say
pass the rum again this way
pour it till the top meets brim
swallow whole then fill again.

Under the Table

Poker player's mind will float
where the chair leg stood and wrote
watching back with its arm
it writes a cheating note.

Fonsetorigo

Has come to say
the poems of Sally
will not pass away.

The Eye of Origin

The sorrel with pleasant-tasting leaves
will grow beyond the looker's eye
so impaired upon the page of power
it leaves to wink at each hour.

The Flues' Observant Note

Smoke it passes leaf of tree
winds round limb so bark can't see
then leaves on arms of breeze
to fall apart as it may please.

The Limit of the Limerick

Under whichever circumstances
thoughts seem to have themselves to chance
however far the mind might go
is what we find so few little know.

Selected with Care

The time has channeled the waters deep
to where the poetic secrets no longer keep
the mind in constant stare and maze
as was often done in olden days
a surf would work his way toward spire
with flames that burnt the verses higher
what brought the thought that all knowledge knew
was kept inside so often few.

Empty Verse

Now turns the page with reader's eye
with parts they wish to not pass by
they read on over what's past been read
to never hear what one might have said
it is somehow the better way
for often words have not much to say.

Head Stall

How empty some lives do grow in the
    field with no life to sow
Afraid to look and search on out
Living in a sphere they know is doubt
Not hungry to favor their own food for thought
They more often wish that they were not
Or know no better of the open rhyme
They live this life to not ever often find
That all things that are Are
of the mind.

The Cost of Tomb

No price could ever be too high
for each soul and spirit knows there is one
    that will meet its eye
deep or shallow or in the air
all will have one so that they might care
soon in coming or in distant time
don't look for yours nor neither mine.

Owlet

As owls stare through the night's cool air
not knowing who has come near or close to there
they turn their head then wink their eye
as hand does point toward them to fly
they ask not when or even why
but who suggests for them to leave
is one not wise to disbelieve
in all the feathers that they assume
nestled about so they might plume
the thoughts that run throughout the wood
they all would have if they all but could.

Companion

The writer who does not know his pen
is his nearest and most dearest friend
has lost the tune the song would write
which plays most often on through the night
to ears that hear only within the mind
the notes of the creative line
that takes the eyes and thoughts away
and under its spell where it will say
unto each reader large or small
there be no way to see it all
unfolding words that wind as trail
that lead onto the final tale
told by this poet one
who writes with night but waits for sun
to meet the path that's proved its place
and left for others its verse to face.

Lovelorn

Eyes of silver, thoughts of gold
repeating everything that you're told
young and innocent made to pay
often giving all away
power fails then will succeed
taking all that you need
I've met you now on paper line
there are no rules we need to find
as smoke flies on and floats in air
it shows us how it does not care
the words of people, heart, and soul
are only things we think we know
if all was cleared and passed away
there would still be one thing I'd have to say
I love you

Lost

Willows weep with wine
tear drops fall from the sky
roots in clouds that twist like twine
woven round the written line
a mystery falls with the rain
sinking deep in fear
a pool is formed and you look in
to see your answer clear.

The Obvious Oaf

Bitter, backward, worn-out mind
made to last a short time
thinks of treason, dwells on hate
has no good thought to relate
adds with failure, counts with line
all his answers you can find.

Comet

Patterns put to please their plot
wanting what they've never got
staring stars that sing in sky
catching all the people's eye.

Saliva of Death

Spit that's spewed from mouth and spat
upon the floor near the threads of mat
disgust and greed grows more than fat
as night drools on the back of day
pathogen will meet its prey.

Clockwork

The eyes on face with hands that move
only have one time to prove
one or twelve, whichever be
is not for us to stop and see
passing by a moment's breath
we live a life to meet a death
breathing out across our space
leaving thoughts no one will trace
they gather here and make their place
as if to say we need not chase.

Flowery

Wilted roses with passed-out powers
tears that fall more than showers
completed colors gone from flowers
alive in life for only hours
music marching a musty mile
that will not reach the gruesome pile.

Captain of the Current

Moving waves with wind that knows
all the ways the water goes
turns toward shore then out to sea
the current makes its own way free
past the ship that sails from sand
its waves of wonder will understand
below the surface to ocean's floor
the voyage it makes is always more
than anyone has sailed before.

Goods and Services

A rune in tune
once played too soon
a secret in its own sight
an epicene material world
spinning through the night
has stopped to see
itself free
of course on which it's set with origin
inside its core
to cast out its final debt.

The Eve of War

Bullets fly as thoughts explode loaded in the mind
hired and fired at targets many, leaving life behind
dead as gone, dust that blew
past the open door
all who call, stand, and fall
beneath the wary floor.

The Symptom of Suggestion

When the mind flows with ink on page
the source of creation is bound with rage
the wheels of the mill have turned out the grain
while leaving the field free of its pain.

Stoic Is the Storm

The window opens on toward the sky
then on ourward looks the eye
past the clouds the thunder sounds
to where the cosmic heart pumps and pounds
past the tears the lightning will go
into the minds of those who know.

A Good Fit

When what is done slows down a bit
and things are made to more simply fit
the sky will clear of clouds with rain
and lives will live more free of pain
like setting suns that burn the day
we see through words that wish to say
that none of us have found our way.

Die Weeping

Deadly honest, seriously shy
open minds wonder why
with treetops growing toward cloudy sky
catching raindrops in every eye
leaves the conclusion all must cry.

Rhythmic Fluctuation

As the tree has changed in form
through winter spring and raining storm
so the limbs and lungs will fill
with air that can't stay still
the morning brings them news that they might
often have to use as a gift or tool of time
they both will breath inside this rhyme.

Aloof

Over the hills runs a free tale
how men out at sea hunt for the whale
under the water lives a new line
that catches the meaning written most fine
fisherman of folly fighters of fun
deal from the bottom of the deck where there is none
to be lonely for a new story poem
as the heroes imagine themselves are alone.

Veil of Depreciation

I see the mask slip from your face
much too large to stay in place
out looks the eye of sly retreat
with unreal thoughts from head to feet
they sprinkle on the ground as rain
to fill each day with constant pain
a stolen mystery not yet solved
as how the world has evolved
answers on the written page
bring the crowds to constant rage
excited over rules that spoil
past the point that blood would boil
thicker than the crust of earth
all matter lost its little worth.

Silently Well-Spoken

A tailor of the words they say
how they speak but seldom pay
which is more to have in hand
a castle made of dreams or sand
a rose or orchard in the night
both look the same without the light
till morning comes and picks but one
overnight has just begun
to decide its final choice
will not be said with human voice
the beauty of the star and sky
are only two that can tell why
the choice is made the flower knows
it calls itself both white and rose
rose for life, love, and death
it will say all three within one breath.

Upon the Field of Verse

Tales of truth will often change
to where they appear much more than strange
no figures add to round it off
as life remains more hard than soft
we minus memories, years, and time
till we are left with just one line
describing how the world would say
all things have been but not to stay
stumbling, crying, falling down
off to where the end is found
inside the drama, act, and play
is how the timeless hollow game
lives on so well without a name.

Understand the Sun

Terror turns a page in tale
told to those who often fail
at finding flowers growth
with sun and water we call both
evening waits to send its sleep
to stems and roots running deep
in a vase now on the table
sits a beauty hard to label
given to a heart to know
what will make the feeling grow

The Natural Stream

A spinning world that never shows
around in space how much it knows
of lives that look and live then die
that always question and wonder why
one answer waits to tell in time
how most will never ever find
a meaning to the riverbed
where it will sleep and rest its head
its mouth says always to the sea
that it has come to simply be.

The View

Sun sets on your shoulder, morning waits to rise
as the day gets older, midnight meets your eyes
Love is a riddle in the verse, the surfs and king will say
repeated from the jester who juggles lives away
the newest of the hours has seen the past cut down
as the ivory towers cast shadows on the ground
where the meeting started and who first cast the eye
is never brokenhearted, he will always fly.

The Eyes of You

Your thought to me is precious and
    how it leaves your mind
to share with me a moment the things we both will find
are counted in our memory where no one seems to see
how each day has brought you closer knowing more of me
as simple as the feathers on wing that always flies
the answer to our love comes shining through your eyes.

Death Watch

Magic mystery about your eyes
leaves you left with no surprise
only when the next one dies
you will grow that much more wise.

Ha Ha

When your breath meets the torn-up tide
undecided where you may ride
think more than once what melts the ice
or you may have to pay the price.

You Can't Win Them All

You speak, you win, you choose, you lose
you know some days are bound to rain
you just walk on and feel no pain
like lakes that form with the sky
the spirit moves out through the eye
with each glance the sun will take
the clouds will move and start to break
the pages weak tear from the book
the strongest ones have made you look.

The Avant-Garde Will Decide to Vanish

Territories never seen beyond all thought or any dream
characters that live in flame
burning past all things the same
acting as the fire of force
calling life to its first source
they leave the space that wills invade
by not referring to what was made
they spy and watch as answers fade
upon a level that's planeas clear
they more than often disappear.

Songster Meets the Soothsayer

Inside the pillow waits a dream
to crawl within the head it's seen
on the shoulders with one wing
above the clouds then everything
he had put himself once there
where nothing caused the air to stare
only round the open space
were few others he could trace
to land more safe than any bird
was at this point somehow unheard
no voice or vision had made this time
only this poem that reads to rhyme.

Dead Line in Hate Ash Bury

When your lines all seem down
turning you back around
forgetting where you once went
or even why you were sent
to each end that has a sign
saying things are just fine
until your thoughts all go in line
to tunnels carving out of sight
always darker than the night
hiding travels of the town
where wisteria is often found
always as the answer ends
told in secret among friends
in the summer next to spring
with lots of words that mean nothing
making clouds dark and gray
that break apart to wash the day
clean of hidden dirty lies
looking out through human eyes.

The Harp

How the yard grows so grave
filled with lives it could not save
marked at head with stone to read
of a life that lived with speed
moved itself upon the plane
where hours passed without the pain
pain of knowing what was slow
pain of showing how little know
when the sun meets the moon
the notes they play are all in tune
a song of death for some too soon.

Parchment Parade

Silhouettes that sit on line
surrounded slightly with red sunshine
words with faces start to smile
but only for a short while
serious as the Sabbath day
when black is worn for passed away
people who had once known time
now have their profiles on the line.

The Solicitor of Solitude

In a marble castle made of stone
lives one mind so all alone
the drawbridge reaches over waters deep
where thoughts are drown and put to sleep
a closing day with sun and moon
has ended now a bit too soon
awake the mind starts to walk
but with no one it has to talk
of the silence setting in
to where the fog has never been
above the shoulders in the head
now hear this mind what words are said
you who think you're all alone
will soon hear the words of stone
making walls we stand all day
to keep the world outside away
tired of the human traits
we've locked them out with iron gates
blisters on their actions few
with simple little bits to do.
they wonder how they've been made
to carry on with lives they'd trade
the story rattles through his head

as though spoken by the dead
alive one day to make this speech
beyond the limit one could reach
a specter stands to point out sound
his voice has spread now all around
as if to make the mind explode
forgetting all that it's been told.

Never Landing

Sit and write till moon turns blue
to think of words strong and true
while waiting for the snow to melt
we see more now just how we felt
together two as moon leaves night
all hours spent without the light
through the dark of distant dawn
the verse was made to carry on
trials and piles with holes in mind
go unnoticed hard to find
a true word told next to a lie
leaves all to hear and stop to try
as all that's said will soon pass by
these wings of love will always fly.

Valentine

Saints with hearts have come to rhyme
in February at the same time
a day to wonder and to show
all the love in heart we know.

Rest Easy

When time ticks by, refusing not to sleep
we'll be together for more than ever
where narrow minds can't see
that things are not as they may seem
our love is more than any dream.

Opinion of Intentions

If one explains the world to you
as rogues and gypsies try to do
with fortunes from the crystal ball
about the walls that never fall
built so high they cannot see
beyond what often has to be
the simple treasure most of all
stands neither short or even tall
sometimes hardest most to find
inside your head a thing called mind.

Clandestine Will

Made of magic, mold, and dust
how soon the jewels have learned to rust
where once a hand could hold the shine
beyond all light and word in time
but where it finds itself again
is wrapped around the quill and pen
pushed to depths of wonder deep
to where the secret verse will keep.

The Gravest Gray Matter

Desire of death, desire to ride
taste of blood then suicide
down on tar the treads have wrote
the will of those who would not note
what it is that makes the glide
the love of death and love of ride.

Land of the Lost

Past the pasture on the range
where words are woven more than strange
with tumbleweed that flies about
wind will lift the meaning out.

Light Energy

Tales that turn the lips to ice
forcing ones to pay their price
with hearts that bleed and pour out pain
left beside the road in rain
they beat their way towards town of tin
where roofs call chimneys off the wind
windows watching at the road
tell the sun it must explode
upon the floor once through the pane
to spread about the room again.

Cryptic Cruise

Ships at sea with women free to roam the docks and pier
night sets in
with deadly sin
still they have no fear
sailor cries
the wind has eyes
that see the port come near
as all is told
it now grows old
and brings the crew to tear
down the cheek onto the deck
the ship is headed toward its wreck
upon the rocks of riddle
a clever answer
has no one to give
not just a little.

Shilly-Shally

Trolls that trip and change in form
never caring right or wrong
they leave the mountain toward the sea
to fish the bottom so it may be
they catch the meaning put below
what others wish most not to know.

Early Death

A visit from the sun on line
is all the trolls where left to find
walking toward the coast of sea
where ships had sailed to waters free
free of knowing saying when
as all paraded with paper, pen
a hand moved to spell its fate
telling of its will too late
married to the sun and moon
the days would change all too soon
as lives collapsed upon the shore
they washed away forevermore.

Dead Soldier

The empty flask stood up to ask
whose lips have drank me dry?
I'll search the room
till it turns to tomb
and crack within their eye
for my last drop
they would not stop
so now they all must die
they've thrown my label
beneath the table
and spit back in my guts
not just men lost me as friend
but even many sluts.

War Bonnet

Everlasting war of death
battled out with generals' breath
beat the bullets in their flight
sliding silent through the night
know the army with all its names
caught-up caution played as games
said as secrets told to some
kept by those who wish they won.

Like Clockwork

When work is done and winding down
no one left rushing round
carried hours out the door
on the clock they live no more
watched they were for part of day
now they're gone far away.

Observation

Watch your mind
watch your word
speaking to the one who's heard
live inside the pen and page
see them grow without age.

Undecided

Bound-up
round-up
rolling pen
finds its mark to make again
blown-up
torn-up
tatted truth
told inside a betting booth
sour
bitter
sweetest tooth
sharpest point points at you
wondering what is next you'll do.

History

Over battered bodies rides
horse of Indian searching guides
underneath the hoof skull hides
many secrets of their tribes.

Facade

Next time you disappear don't wonder why
just ask yourself when you should try
to be gone over where there is not
everything you never have really got.

Far Sad

Here I sit deep and lonely
the voice I hear is mine only
depths can go just so far
only as they seem they are.

Flame

Candle burns deep and slow
knowing where it has to go
people think that they're deep
with their secret they can't keep.

Mystery

As tomorrow breaks at dawn
don't be looking far too long
for what there is you cannot see
deep inside you or me.

Mountain

Past the present still lives now
no one knowing ever how
catch the thought your mind just had
be it good or be it bad
all of them one life can't count
how they ever do amount.

Eye Spot

As your eyes are disguised blue, brown, and green
always thinking what they've seen
wink, blink, and cry
heavy stare wondering why
tear drops on the floor
looking out the corner for more
when it comes to an end
they've closed for sleep once again.

Perpetuity

When you're falling forever slow
through a life no one can ever know
wish to explain the point you've lost
the price of life has no cost
when you're climbing up the page that was
    torn from your book
think how others had to look
through each line that has them peer
at the page that will not disappear.

Fletch

Newfound fables switch their facts
when the train has jumped its tracks
over to the waiting station
is their name and occupation
written on the wall with pen
are the follies of all men
ink has dried with humor lost
just when you think you've got it made
in comes the poet to pull the shade
takes your sun to the outside
holds you in where you will hide
looks you close in the eye
as you look back you then know why.

Literature

To revolutionize the world is to deny it
of its natural inability to think
bring it to conclusions
with ink
and optical illusions
of life there is no other way
one can speak the start to say
what they thought they saw today.

Gambling Hell

Shuffle your mind before you play your mental card
always deal from the bottom line no matter how hard
cut the deck and not your thoughts
and you'll receive more than lots.

Letter Opener

The wind turning pages
lost numbers and paragraphs punctuated with meaning
the sand slipping over sentences, letters leaning
mailed, written, read
torch burning at ending with the message it's sending
the stamp is disqualified just for pretending

Lost Law Hand

As the law is turned around
spoken only where it's found
only those who sat and wrote
noticing the song lost a note
who will say what's left to read
always spoken to those who need
anarchy does wear its face
seldom seen or out of place
either one for them the choice
neither one without a voice.

Ascensive Power

Stale crumbs of words in the kitchen garden
calling to hallways of verse, empty into the purse
of meaning worse
original ourlet as in ever
lines that tell of knowing whether they will meet the eye
till then they're never as a thought
once their freshness could be caught.

Together

Blue hollowing out the valleys
fog resting on the hillside
or is it dew collecting on the blades of grass?
you have seen this happen
all in nature's smile
where we can rest a while
without once seeing the sky cry
we all have little cause without each other's reply.

Overboard

The plank walks itself to sea air
the ship has lost its sail
folded in the galley
held for bail
top mast peeks from under pail
sailor picks up words
with bowsprit in his teeth
how will it fit on the deck
the ending holds the hand of wreck.

Ship Wheel

Silver near the island dock
silkworms weaving
the patchouli smell slides on the oil
the memory leaves pavilions with pavanes
as pirates push through burning doors
to escape the treasure of who explores
the rubies on the hand at sea
will soon sail their ship toward me
with wavelength piracy.

Dreamland

Do they expect the fruit has been eaten?
on the next line they'll be meeting
not one repeating
it's over till the tide say high
out we go
in it comes so slow
washing back what we think we know
the new breeze fresh on the line
runs whale with stream even though it would seem
it's never more than this dream.

Brief Bookman

Tired as the ink dries
the stone whets itself on the shore
words of wind blow once more
taken from the cloud they rain
never missing any pain
they still float
on the hand that's often wrote
so much in just a little note.

Life

Vibrissa the cat is frisk
a rodent runs its rail
not as the cat could fail
the sweep with final claw
tears mouse open raw
with back of neck in its jaw.

Attraction with Fraction

Like a stomach you grow full
of the words that start to pull
your attention is not so great
till you have known your fate
I could sit and read your palm
or some other bible psalm
whichever one interests you
of them both I've read a few
honest in my magic game
like no other plays the same.

Grave Decision

Sepulchre of the wicked
holding out its arms
whet your physical priggish prima donna
who moves the night
your eye, ear, and sight.

Difficult Decision

When the sweat pours like rain
you'll really know it's work again
who designed this world to turn
with many minds that never learn?

Proportionality

Reading, writing, worn-out pen
spelling words once again
over hills of meaning came
walking old man with a cane
pointing toward the lake of doubt
with his stick he pointed out
errors in the sky were made
covered by the clouds of shade
perfect is this sun that shines
reflecting of the lake then pines
taking dark from the earth
giving life its total worth.

Present Present

Kill the past and bury deep
or it will have you often weep
though the future has its spell
now is better just as well.

Open Sesame

If you have read my opened mind
tell yourself what you could find
in the depths of love and hate
artive most people much too late
to see the game of opposite
is nothing more than what you get.

March

Onward bier rolls toward town
parade that follows wears its frown
as the fair will start next noon
singing such a hollow tune
the ear of death will learn their call
but no one has concern at all.

The Handwriting

Teeth that turn to tooth and say
how have you chewed this life away?
will soon be found beneath the pillow
wiping tears with weeping willow
songs that turn their backs on you
will be sung by little few
days that live no more than now
have all been lived so long somehow
as each verse has come to you
you stand again to see on through.

Quixotic Conduct in the Castle

Have you thought the words could be an invisible history
of what you thought you could see coughing
        to the smoke in air
where there is no one to compare their force and place
had been written on your face
without its mask which facade you might ask
dead as the day that has gone past where soldiers play
as knights pass by the world is explained in your eye.

The Thing

Camouflage of consciousness from the buds of spring
never show all they bring
canopy of green
hiding what may be seen
on the shelf of earth
sits the book of birth.

Again

When every poem has been read
and every word has been said
stopped and taken back
then all explains what it does lack.

Inside

A paleomilitia attitude inside her mind
did grow stepping on to the line duty left
    to those unknown
and how the words lost their gravity but never their sound
travelers to the you-know-where
a place she never found.

More Doorways

Here I am, a door
not listening anymore
to feet upon the floor
I could shut you in
closing often
making the sounds thin
how nice to be a door
if it makes you love me more.

More Headway

Suspended in the height of stupidity
the last frontier once intelligence notably
acquired itself a fluke in the presence
of plagiarized ideas that mold and ferment in the cellars
of some nervous tissue above the neck of knowledge.

Heady

Becoming undone in settlements of silence
    and word choice
has no one spoken of enigmas
who've broken burning in the night
with gold compounded offering disguised
might premature as incompetence
with lackadaisical empty sense.

Headstone

On the grave of death despair
in the yard just over there
comes the spirit who will not save
ruling from the sky and grave
words were written on his rock
you will not listen as he will knock.

Headstream

Source of river as it will flow
past the words we will not show
from the start it runs its course
without it there is no force
down it as we seldom float
in the poems that we've wrote.

Crash

Dust the bars they all did close
since the day noticed rose
on the tomb of sweet and sour
drinks were drunk by the hour
toward the time that fun did end
all the damage would not then mend.

Dreamy Music

Dark and morbid eyes of blue
in the skull of little few
depression set to dance on hope
so no other may ever cope
with the sense of life and death
blowing out the final breath.

Most Wicked

Glass that finds its bottom fast
thinks of drink that did not last
mirror that reflects just age
has cracked itself with hanging rage
pen that's lost all its ink
will no longer write or think
well that's run so deep then dry
ask the cloud to stop and cry
people with their heads held high
question answers they don't know why.

Autumn

Carry back the wind to trees
where it left leaving leaves
on the ground to pile and blow
in the air they wish to go
onto limbs where once was birth
knowing all their blooming worth
as the leaf has stopped to live
the tree next year will still give.

See

What have you gathered
as your thoughts they collect
and your secrets cannot be kept
candle burns with mind of own
as music listens for its tone
people live and so few see
through their mind with purity
sad it seems but who's to say
what secret trick this life will play.

Power Dive

Lose the game and keep your mind
either of the two will find
you have started on your way
to learn how others wish that they could play.

Power Blind

Deeper burns the flame of truth that few wish to face
taken from the wick it's lost, missing in its place
shallow can the game be played without a second try
still circles find the people go never seeing why.

H. A.

Light that opens up this door
has never turned its key before
through the webs of wanting space
travels it without a trance.

New Wizard

Diversified novelist write to the moon
might the rhetoric beguile them soon
blue flower with white noon
has its veil unfold in tune.

Sharp-Witted

With their ideas so shallow and their concepts so deep
our newborn thought they will not reap
once they decide to fathom out each brain
    cell inside their skull
they'll see that it's somewhat dull.

How Else

End of road comes again
however long it could pretend
start of day will find its path
riding toward the sun of wrath
on wings of bird we seldom fly
but never more than with our eye.

Fly

Nest is made where they may stay
until they learn to fly away
falling from the limb with flight
now has taught them that they might.

Mélange

Can this hold a point in time?
a pen and page that will not rhyme
an eye that will not follow line
is better shut and left behind.

Conclusion

In the depths of this page
are there words locked in a cage?
when you put the key in door
turn it past the line before
you take your final look
at what is the end of book.

The Bar Czar

The Delight of Creativity

The bardic bloom is hidden well
and few in tune caress its spell
double takes are not often made
and crude mistakes create the shade
though deep inside, each coven cone
there is a light of constant lore
flickering lantern now holds still
that we may read the gypsies will
across the glade we'll glide
and unfold with them
to understand what's moved
their quill and pen

Christened with a Fainthearted Fortune

Bedazzle the slowness and shadows
Bring them to speed
A curse and good tidings
Both will the witch use and have need
While Beelzebub bounces and brings on our own vice
The flocks call for his head and will pay any price
The offerings are many beneath their tall steeple
And evil has sunk deeply inside of these people
Though secret and hidden
From their purest mind's eye
They too wish for the end, the day one will die

Serpents and Flames

Cockatrice and stares us down
Though only in legend has it been found
Fiction is fathomed to not make the score
On the temple's charge behind a locked door
Now it has risen and dangles the truth
'til it is caught beneath the dragon's tooth
Pulled by a knight on a mission from shire
To spread through the village catching on fire

If You Should Believe

A small satiric poet from the grove
Came to village
And with one verse he drove
All of mankind to the sallow swamp
Where the water witch did wait to haunt
Every thought that did leak from them
They could not hid not near pretend
Once her verse and curse had covered all
They headed back through their cities wall
To realize their second savior's glance
Was on three sorcerers and not by chance

Crystal Gazer

Let the crescent moon shine
Down through these windowed walls
It sings a changing tune
That shawls the thoughts of all.
Then sit beside the crystal ball
That whispers won't you look
The future, I'll tell to you more clear
Than any written book.

The Wing Tips

Tall blades surround the blackbird
Winnowing past its wings
It hears the traveler's tune of esoteric things
Learning all the lore of what the song has chimed
It flew deeper in the core
Of tales that clearly rhymed
To each one it listened long and never gave away
The morals or the meaning to anyone who'd say
"I've learned this from the blackbird
Through all legends it has flown
And all their deepest meanings
To me they're clearly shown"

Demeter Before

First discovered largest,
Ceres be our god
Spread across the earth
With the harvest of sod.
She flaunts the flowers and grain
And the herbs just as well
While she lies in the heavens
To cast the growing spell.

Perhaps in Time

What so-called scholars have surely forgot
Is sorcerers speak in rhyme more than not
Nor have their halls of ivy taught them well
How to cast or understand their own spell.

Work Inside the Cirque

Rhapsodize the elephant's ear
For it is the largest and needs to hear
Words that soothe its memory clear
Of times on trails that had no fear

Ewer Pouring the Wine

During flagrante delicto scribing
The pen's anger becomes more inflamed
For the fact that its masters may never be tamed
"Please write of beautiful peace
And the kindness of mankind.
Why must you move me through the darkness so blind?
May I never have the pleasure of one sympathetic day
when you use me for poetic passion and play."

Following the Freshness of Style

Inside our shell we've waited to hatch
With a tale we can tell no other might match
One that is new, steadfast, and bold
Never once repeated or thought to be old
Though soon the shine dims
And off comes the polish
That all wish to keep
Declaring the wisdom has not been so deep

Meltingly Mention the Magic

When Merlin's mad and upset with their spite
He strolls through the study later at night
Knowing their petty ill will
Is caught in towering thirst
With nothing to spare
The likes of their constant curse
Only his whim and his wish will pervade
Melting away mistakes that they have made

Rays Through the Clerestory

Listen clearly to what is sung,
Off the tip of thine own tongue.
Time, it's fooled into moving where
You cannot tell it does prepare
To sing and sound with verses round
That swallow surely what they care.
Lo! The deepest pain that has been set
Was done with words some did regret,
And the clearest light one might see
Is brother to the poetry.

Please Sing the Master

Chalet down beside them.
Has one door full of ivy vines
It shall open up its windows
To hear blossoms speak in rhymes
We may not unravel the riddle
That the sorcerer speaks on through
Though for sure when near the riddle
He know we're trying harder too

To Have Their Minds Read

Cockles of the heart are more of the mind
Just as the truth of anything you'll find
And those that make the most of it
One well-known to perfectly fit
All of the pieces of the Magian maze
Into the puzzle we work on these long days

Fog Bows

The fog and mist they both hold hands
Clinging to the lower hands.
Practiced at the art of disappear
They tell each other no one can hear,
When we'll set, or when we'll rise
Has meaning only to the eyes.
And the wind that sets behind them too,
Can never quite see clearly through

No Longer A Secret

Close-knit the cape that we sorcerers wear
Changing the shape beneath the locks of our hair
Down on cloud nine, they mull in elation
We've heard each word of their conversation
They do not see us or have any idea
That we know of their uncontrollable fear

Woven in the Bedstraw

What clauses this spell
has hidden from thee.
The white light and candle
below we both see.
Winds flicker flame
and leave dry the land.
Still the sage and his sentence
We do not understand.
When the mystery leaves lonely
With no one at its reach.
Backward it will read
And more powerfully teach.
How many thoughts has the mind one day?
Where do they begin?
And at night, where might they lay?

Curiosity of the Lyrics

Spire as the wand
that waves toward your head
Placing the spell
as you sleep in your bed
Craftly is thee
that the dream has begun
Which collides with the tune
the choirs never sung
The clandestine chorus
is draped in desire
To learn of the message
its scale will inspire

Recall the Pillow Sham

Has the sheet not been your closest cover
When dreams drip down the walls
To dredge out fantasies
il beard tongues wake you frantic
That the penstocks will not free
The water that they need to grow so lovingly

Brilliant Qualities

The tall coven-tree shades at times
The witch who's best at working rhymes
Beneath its limbs
She weaves the cape
For winter's winds that will come late.
The seasons know her hand's not cruel
That form the growth of nature's not cruel.
Though many never sight her ways
And have not thought,
What fills her days?
She still maintains the garden's glory
Tells best of what's in her story.

Moon Deems Our Destiny

Cock crows break us from our spells
As we hear the tolling of the knells.
Now another no longer here dwells.
Tonight's moon will watch his spirit rise,
No tears will shed from its golden eyes.
For long before the time of man
It was placed high to understand.
That the ways inside our mind so the
Often changed below its yellow shine.

It's Not The Lift, It's The Sort

Bows jest atop the presents
They pleasantly adorn,
The paper beneath their knots
Will soon be cast and torn,
The gift it might be mammoth
Or of the small variety,
But in the thought of giving
Is where receiver's eyes should see.

The Art Casting

Stakes upon the contingency
That the mind will soon start to see
With its own opening elusive eye
How clearly
Spells are cast into the sky
To spread and reflect
Off the earth's one moon
That will set each season in perfect tune
'tis from the meadows and the forest deep
This rhyme has come for us to always keep

Special Collection

OWL WONDER WHO

The Competition

"I was just checking,"
Said the Queen to the Pawn,
"What this day
You have had your mind thereon."
"My dear it is the castle
Cross the field they call a board.
Most sly waiting to show you
It's the victorious Lord."
Wil'st turning her finest crown
To see the drawbridge free from the gate
And the woe to be captured
Surely she must most certainly hate.

From the Creator of Curiosity

Wonder, weep, the start to die
Poems will catch the beggar's eye
Staring at the queen and more
Kings just want their even score

Wicked Withershins

Quicksand in the hourglass,
leading us astray.
Stealing precious moments
from our magic day.
Lobo howls at the heavens,
They have not given him his prey.
Perdition points out clearly,
It will soon be sauntering his way.
The drama drops degrees
To where the mind is froze.
While the warlocks work with wisdom
That no one ever knows.

One Joke Gone Wild

Played and worn
Then bet and bounced
Below the table once pronounced
Like a will that would collect
The only jewel to meet neglect

Having Luck Making Ducks and Drakes Of

Poetic phantoms who search
The gavel beacons lead
With common and patent logs
Telling of an unknown speed
Where white stone towers
Lit the coastal med
Then well-taught tars of Tartarean greed
Swelled up from the ocean's own sunken heart
With all their wild, wet, whiskers and whispers
Telling why the world did finally start

Techniques of the Drama

Countless the castles craving their king
Endless the notes the birds have to sing
Voiding the high and lowest degree
Ways of the woods the wizard will see
Who had them bound to musical mote
Hayden and Handel never once wrote
More simple symphonies
In so striking their sound
Though readers have listened
They have not paid a pound.

Open Lich Gates

Grog shop with barrels empty
Tender loading up a cart
Hears the campanile calling
The morning to its start.
The bell its toll for many
While the mask is caught in mold
Brass eyes are forming
Of the one with rum who fought the cold.
Losing battles with the winter
The frozen gutter took his life
Helped by spirits from the tavern
Who twist the stolen sunken knife.
Broken blade inside his back
Buried deeply and so proud
Then placed neatly in the yard
Claiming plots that make a crowd.

Your Diglot Verse

This direful life, its length does pretend
As glamorous death rests round each bend
Crawling past the chambers, hung with one bell
We learn of the truth in who casts the spell
Reading the Opus till it sings in sleep
Telling of secrets no costumes could keep.

The Better of the Lot

We've been known to dwell
Well in the spell
Of a moment or maybe two
Like lovers roam in the grass
Before it grew or knew of dew.

Cross-Threaded

The floor it meets the ceiling
The walls they run and hid
The bars they have no feeling
While holding in the pride
Dust it will make the moments
While there upon the broom
As the bodies slowly rot
Inside their covered tomb
A skull it speaks to courtyards
Where juries take a break
Thinking that their melted minds
Have made a big mistake
They shiver at the counsel
And shake on towards the bench
Like lost nuts that have no bolt

Nor perfect fitting wrench.

Hearing the Pitch-Dark

When their balance becomes off-pace
They fall and bleed upon the floor
Where we once walked and talked for more
Now no more bottles make the rounds
And sips are few that may be found
A sober high has taken on
All the cries that once came out wrong.

Poor Trade at Sea

Now on a ship the parrot swings
His perch it waves through and sings
"You foolish sailors have no course
From empty islands comes your force
Where no king or queen be your lord
They welcome you with beard and sword
To hide the jewels and polished gold
With tales at sea that can't be told"

Bold Imagination

Confused by the creations
That never come to be
Crowded in the classes
That no history
Obscure the endless madness
Appearing June's early May
While pushing the heat of summer
Further into each one's way

Sticking to the Ribs

Sea swallows up the sands of rhyme
Bees will sting the hands most unkind
Turning pages of tiger's teeth
That taste the blades inside their sheath
Placed by knights who never will kneel
Before the lords who've had them feel
The ways the verse had strolled the queen
Then so amused inside her dream
Deeper than the dark moat outside
The castle where she chose to hid
'neath leaves of her flowery book
The knights were forced to take a look
Yond the power of word and pen
The voices call the list again
Astonished that their names not on
The living list to leave at dawn
Lids grow heavy, lips lisp, then yawn
About their life and adventure
That will no longer carry on

A Big Wig Bootlicker

Beside the yawl the ink horns float
Free from the hand that sank
As slow as it had wrote
Was one who told of kings
Living without despair
Now life sinks below the cold wave
without a thought we'd wish to save
Thinking of the sunken
So clean within their grave

Under the Rose

Hardest to follow and fathom
Impossible to pinpoint clear
All the ruins and the riches
Cast about to now disappear.
The title waves to the stanzas
Written beside the oak
The birch will bend its ear
Though hear now words we spoke.
Four cast the cloak more evenly
A veil our minds have worn
While waiting for the point
That lies above the thorn.

Magnetizing the Flight of Ambition

Dying verse with a meaning
So it somehow understands
Who holds the highest feather
That flies through their grasping hands

Not Drabbing at the Opportunity

Rising from the catafalque of script
The scope finds lines of poison
That make all their visions lose their grip
Upon the foaming future, fearful of its fate
He wrote the constant memories
That vanished through each polished gate
He tamed the ink of centuries
That would have dried soon like a scab
To paint the portrait different
With no colors that would turn drab

Few Near All, Thee Understands

Clandestine correspondence
The reader knows it most well
Inside the witch 'bout to cast her spell
On classmates of the high throne
Far beyond the yellow moon
Predicting absence of the mourning
To have shone up way too soon

To Have Guilt Edging for the Guillotine

The cleaver knows the cuts
On the edge that's hard to bear
When standing inches from it
While it passes through the air
The swath speaks clearly now
As it makes its fine display
'fore forming every figure
Where two separate pieces lay

Thy Crown Is Missing

Hot springs in woods soothe the sounds
As the forest grows
'neath the paws of hounds
Hunting fox and wolves who write
In dens that flicker
With warm candlelight
Lo! Coops of chickens lay their eggs
While sloops of sailors tap their kegs
To toast their king that has turned out
Upon the street to beg and shout

Our Test Tree

Look and find the ways which point with hand
Toward the deeper times we understand
Leave out the leaking ships who love to spy
On tears that never come to wash the eye
Kill but do not bury laws of the crippled crowd
Who will wear their innocence
On their heads so proud
It's only fuel for the fire of poetic time
That burns across these pages
With the warmest rhyme

To Throw Away What You Will

You know those cloudy, misty days
When people change their callous ways
You've seen the sun burn hot the deluxe lands
While poor thirsty farmers throw up their hands
Till rain hits the wilting crops
Counted by how long it drops
Hungry hammers clawing nails
'neath the wish of more mares' tails.

Who We Are

The gentle reminders
Our memory sure needs
As the ego more often
Should pull up its weeds
If our mind is a garden
Let's let it be plowed
Then carefully planted
With a strong seed that's proud
If our feet spread so wide
And more giant our step
Let's go back to the line
That won't let us forget.

Brut Tall Eyes

Hiding in the secret (brunes) of memory
They bathe in the dragon's blood
While drying by the fire
The model madness cakes upon boots as mud
Then gives gold to the most enchanted liar.
Still bellows fill, light the lungs
Of an army planned to die
Then marauders make their moves
Slicing cake into a pie.

Moving the Cornerstone

Poor creature, such a beggarly fellow
Jaundice set in his eyes turning yellow
Good health on a curbstone
Cures for the earth
Though no sickness in sight
Shall loose of its worth

Try Angles of Talent

Once ripe the reader's eye is stolen
From its socket in a spell
To the windward point of paradise
Where our wizards wait to tell
The wicked warlocks warn us of doom
As warriors weep for widows
That I married men, far too quick and soon
Wordplay it does love the pun
The sharp tail uses for its support
Like Lake Poet's lost in lust
Who wrote for ladies they would court
Their style is not inside here
We know they numbered three
Still on their island thinking
Of poetic history

The Pure Argot That Steals

A science to the language
A history to the thought
A written poem inside us
That no one has yet forgot
The memory made beneath
Climbing through each magic man
Close to the power of learning
So we may understand
The clockwork of the mind
That springs unto the command
Which rules the rich and poor
By one influential hand

Spooling with the Thin Thread of Life

The needle it's waiting
For its one eye to see
Which stitches take it through
The hems of poetry

The Creator of Their Illness

Youth, it once had us
Naive in its spell
Walking through the wild
With tales we would tell.
Now age bends us over
And walks us more slow
Still the ways of our lives
They never will know.
They would like to look in
And take part of our gain
But as soon as they do
Their minds do go insane.
With them we will tamper
And then toss them a treat
That if they should come near
They will die 'fore our feet.
Now back there they sit
And think what's been said
Knowing they could not have thought
Without the words they have read.
We weave them like blankets
To hold bold out the cold
On one side they lie frozen
While more warm we grow old.

A Naked Sword Finds Dullness

The teachers eat the apples
Placed poison upon their desks
The students gather at the funerals
To finish off their fast test.
The tailor sews the trousers
Of tyrants that never fit
All pieces of the puzzle
In the mysterious pit.
Finding the fifteen events with Mary
Is our crafty life and trade
That sees enigmas forming
And knows just how that they were made.

Our Far Bet Is Larger

No sense in brooding over the past and its pits
Neither falling inside
Where the watch throws her fits
Either in landing the ancient old spell
That has turned all the chimes
Into a ringing bell
It could be the farmer who thought of his cow
Off in the field he had forgotten to plow
It may be the sailor walking the plank of a ship
For not mending a sail that a hard with did rip
Through we know it was the jeweler
Who did not set the stone
Thrown hard at the giant
That merely had him moan

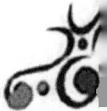

Poor Traits in the Gallery

Our reason and thought can be twisted to no end.
Feelings and emotions do not live in the pen.
These pages have taken hearts from the minds
Looking for loves in the hardest of times.
Our pleasure and power often hold hands
O'er the failures that make their commands.
Art and its beauty never looked quite the same
After drinking the wine
That has turned on the game.

Mythological Flyers

What a dire fool Daedalus
He built his labyrinth well
For all that never taught his son
Of heights that know no hell
Well-waxed his wings
Of friendly fowl
In flight they turned to melt
'fore the landing was known
Or ever really felt

Inside This Arid Society

The designer of the cat's skills,
Decorator of fate and doom,
Has the distant death invader
Now turning gray inside his tomb.
The travelers of the current
And the might North Gulf Stream
See Vikings vanish from the verses
That were not in any spirit's dream.
The buckles on the pilgrims
So high-heeled in sunken boots,
Giving thanks to their children
For they're making swift salutes.
The chiefs they then said nothing
About their church, and its slow hand,
That cleared the nature most quickly
With the sickness of its command.

In the Burning Glass Revisited

We are marbling the leaves of poems inside
And streaking the edges where the essence hides.
They're callously closing in
on the bard's fine plot,
with the last reason concealed
why all wars were fought.
Carrying the weak and wounded minds
To the temples baptized by sunken shrines.
Many cross and angry spears in guts
Were found caught inside wide and deepened ruts.
Then set free by verses, their queen did weave,
After long centuries of insisting
In the blaze that they would never believe.

The Crow's Nest Above It All

Hatchways upon the ship
Lead deep to the belly
In the galley there's bread
Black flies and jelly
Sweet thymes they're rigging
A new woven sail
Near jewels in the shipyard
The pirates flee jail
Quite well planned their capture
The most plunderous feat
To take off the necklace
Of the Queen's Royal Fleet
Not tired of the sea
And its ways we are sure
That soon make us thirsty
And sailing for more

Hung in the Balance

All the riddles unraveled
The rhymes clearly sung
Skull and crossbones
Fall from the flags where they were once hung
Barks upon beauty and wonders of the sea
Be captured by shadows of past history
Scholars of seashells start melting inside
Attempting to take the clouds for a ride
They drip from the reign
Darkness holds tight
Causing their hammocks to hang them that night
Near the crow's nest of fortune
In the fog far out of sight

Our Den Sees

Hope chests hold the future's wish
Anglers hunt the largest fish.
Hammocks have the sleepy swing
There in the galley they no longer sing.
Once the song was long and good
And rang with all the words it should.
Now it's short and not so sweet
With tales of whom we have yet to meet.
A raven waits to make its feed
On all the plans we thought we'd read.
But time, it holds him in his grace
So he may not show his nesting place.

Which Scorn Will Be Delivered

Hair grows and fingernails
The witch who watches never fails
To have her locks high in a bun
Walking down the streets we run
Her lips are wise to every pun
None of her spells may be undone
No matter how hard or heavy cast
They're made by her to always last

Reading an Ink Dot's Mind

We have never meet a Rozzer
Who really knows how to read
They're hung and strung
All about Port Bootle
In their blazers
Two shades of twisted tweed

Speaking Fowl Language

Strong enigmas ending rhymes
Magic minutes escape their times.
When no designs were carved in wood
Was just last year we understood.
While willows weep and hang so low
It's in the way they're shown to grow.
Upstage blood and starch of stone
Right from birth are clearly thrown.
Past swindled songbirds forced to vie
Over crumbs and crowds that crawl and die

With Empty Stomachs

(Thy) pantries ponder pies
Their crust poked neatly forming eyes
Awaiting dinner with hungry cries
Tea kettle blows and brings surprise
To the butler bounding down the stairs
As the banister breaks in several layers
While no one will rescue or even cares

Controlling the Unknown

No wave will unravel
The angle of rhyme
Written to take
The eye and its time
Most poets are lazy
Then worked to the bone
Choosing the words
That sit all alone
So are the answers
Given to them
As the tailor sews down
Their only silk hem

In Dull Gents

The camouflage has been had
Their thoughts may go so high.
Thought everyone has someone
They more sooner wish would die
Trouble it rides the hardest road
Then leads on to calmer days
There never will be anyone
To explain all of its ways
Even the religious must clearly soon admit
There's too many reasons
That simple will never fit
Claim that it is evil
'til the clouds may know no sky
Then never will you see
The love that's within one's eye
Figure it out for sure
and write it upon each line
Though no one will read it
They will never have the time
Terror you presume is part of this mess
Though turn to your mind
And give it one more guess
That there never has been words
To explain all of this life
And there never will be feelings
So sharp as this poetic knife

We Played Your Eyes

People say their hearts beat slow
Until in love or hate
As they quickly do decide
What must become their fate
Fools will make each madman move
Toward towers in the sky
Where patience waits without tears
For it many no longer cry

Two Pair of Lies Their Powerless Speech

The road it travels slowly
Upon itself to find
Where wastrels stop and rest
To let the day unwind.
It passes past the sleeping
With dead and dying dreams
And winds along the rivers
Once formed by all the streams.
It tells more of feet and wheels
That land their toe on time
While ticking toward the poet
That will no longer rhyme.
Right here sleeping like a child
That never reads with sense
To spend inside the village
Surrounded by its fence.
A wall of starving saviors
Nailed up on every cross
Who look for stones and pebbles
That no longer gather moss.

Post-Orbital Thoughts

Trees of love will bend and break
Like hearts that beat without mistake.
Lungs that fill with life and air
We all will own and chance to share.
Thoughts are free though cannot be
Taken out way beyond too far.
Or plans will crumble like dust
Coming down from an evening star.

We Know

He writes, he reads, then takes apart
The verse that weaves around our heart
As pages turn to dust design
Always we look but never find

The Point

The well-trained hound
Makes one toward its game
As bucks have included in their name
The needle needs it
For its seam and lovely lace
Beside the irrelevant it will take its place
Periods and decimals demand of its mark
As it is often lost within the mind and dark

Our Pen Stokes the Mountains of Meaning

As we go along on course
Sailing no parted seas
Lips lose words they wished to speak
Blown free upon the breeze.
Still some have no true taste
For verse and all its heights
Their mind a sunken ship
Of non-poetic frights.
They rush while bows will bust
Upon the rocks of rhymes
Until that once that they have read
The log at night of sailing times.

Those Place Carding the Reality

Most hungry for the answer soon
They look at night on past the moon
The poets know the stars and fires
As tailors trim the suits for liars

In Possession of the Poetic Blindfold

Sharpener always finds the point
The hands outside have failed to grip
Busy in the pies of plenty
Their fingers will finally slip
From the moments of now and then
Keeping secrets inside the pen
Ideas with more power
Than the bullet with its sure aim
Will spread across the fields of earth
A mighty poetic gain
No winners called in crowds of fright
They stay well-hidden from the light
That the masses must never see
For more blind they'll forever be

More Belles Lettres

If all were wise and had little wonder
What makes the clouds share with the thunder
The power of lightning would be in our hands
To strike all the moments back in time
And to right the words most wildest rhyme

His Story Repeats Itsself

The goddess Hours this day is missing
As the seasons sour with Justice fishing
To trade places with the joker's Two
Who've drawn conclusions no one sees through

Jester Fools Them Once

If the seriousness
Catches you in its palm
Pounding your eardrums
With its loudest alarm
Let the warning fade slowly
And seep in the sand
Like ants it will hide
Till it finds its next man
While darkness she's sprawling
With no mercy, just spite
For all of her meaning
No one may ever write

The Eight Ball

Passing the bars where once we did drink
And staggering down sidewalks
With no clear thought could we think
Watching the stars so sober they shine
Down on the earth that treats them unkind
Mad we go march past aged bottles of wine
To kill off the thought winking
That we have been left further behind

Taming the Pit Fowls

Words wipe an eye then walk our feet
Down past some roads they make a street.
They will not stop to let us be
Until they're read and once set free.
Cells within our minds, they do say
They're working hard and colored gray
Tombs inside the granite city
Claim their lives they once thought pretty.
Wives of wise men in desert sand
Build castles tall that soon won't stand.
Why ever has this life become
So soft then hard, like kegs of rum?
Until we drink its final drop
We'll never know where it may stop.
The hours they beat us to the bed
Where all is dreamed and not once read.
Unless there be just one who might
Take these pages on through the night.
Unconscious heaven tells us soon
It may call us within its room.
Though better now we know than then
There's no such place we might pretend.

In the Easy Chair

Take all the words and make them sing
There's nothing better they may do
They've made themselves to often ring
Mystifying more me than you
Spelling them right or even wrong
They find most comfort in a song
Until the poems have taken space
That leave us empty with no trace
We'll call them friends that lead us on
To better days where we'll read on

THE FIFTH WHEEL

Chapter One
The Subjective Claws
of the Empire's Composing Machine

As They Fall in Love

Woe! The cold wind
It wisps past my door
Causing me to sin
Worse than before
Weigh the wild eyes
Now watching them rise and weep
Not to ever surmise the meaning so deep
Call for the poem
And all version that speaks with rime
Growing cold on the window
Where we watch the first time

Iron Tenacity

Whetting roofs with reigning terror
Fair is the blade's regard
It slices through the simple lives
That fear their death be hard

Scales of Tales and Windy Frost

The world of words winds wicked winds
Around this earth that flows and spins
The wizard watchful waits the wreath
That's worn by doors of far beneath
Where we wish inside
With a wivernous breach
For another written will
We must not teach

Upon the Moist Mist Whet the Wisdom of Wolves

Profit and Adventure propel our verse
Although there's no gold
'neath the hasp of our purse
We hoist up the sails
Of our own ship's song
And point out its bow
To be seaworthy and strong
Storms the waves' whip
While calm the shore sights
The moon and its tune
That sings to these nights

Inside the General's Verse

One never knows for sure
What they will come upon for thought
Unless they look behind
And see where always minds are caught
Wishing they had answers
For every question in the book
While turning all the pages
They forget what made them look

Running Knot

Cannons fire and blow broadside
With no parts to float on tide
The memory has bound to sail
While we walk through their wildest tale
A rope yarn knot will release
From 'round ankles at the feast
Where iron cast held for years
'fore it melted in their tears.

On the Printed Mintage of Life

No one may see
With a stolen eye
No one may talk
With a tongue that's gone dry
And no one may sing
Without a tune to come near
Nor never may notes
Cause themselves to appear

De Jeur Imagine Straight

When one might see
Behind the bench the last jury
Deciding with their own delight
Who has to hang with knots drawn tight
We'll slip the noose of nonsense from our neck
And see the systems ship a total wreck

The Law of Diminishing Returns

Fly jesting in the dinette
Still lurking for loaves of bread,
Shy spider in the corner
Completes its catching web;
As words baked upon the table
Line up to be more clearly read;
While hairs of the butler
Fall from his balding head.

Seeing Through the Nerves

A voluminous tale in script
A collector of the bibelots knows
When its time has come near to quit
Elements of sight decompose
And travelers wish they were not on
The ramstam road that they had chose
There all reputations will rise,
After learning of their death
Who work on each view and breath

Sir Pence at the Gate

Gardens greet them in
While flies they give their lie
Flowers see them low
Crawl 'neath all of their strife
Some would tame their move
With a tongue that's a blade
Slicing at the core
Where shame and fear are made
Then cut away his veil
And have his shadow fade

By Duel or Apology

Scouring the rimes for designs,
The frost has made them all write.
Or at least draw the things they saw
While looking through the boundless blight.
How many mind the silky sash,
Which holds them in from blowing wind.
To break their only sight
That sees the reasons
That will not come out
Or never near to what is right.

Lewd Libels

Those privy broken passions,
Cavalier in style.
Pillow, lace, and power
'neath the heads on trial.
Sentenced to the stanza,
Saluting lines of verse.
Without a word or smile
To make it sound less worse.
As thoughts begin to pile,
Like pennies in their purse
That travel every mile
To break the phantom's curse.

Enrolling Fet as a Co-Translator

The fewer the wants
Makes more marked the man
Growing obscure
With the move of his hand
Lifting the veil
Showing free from error
The queen can never decide
Of which two is the fairer
The mirror is glued
By a reflection that's gray
Shattering at night
With the image of its prey

To the Minds Entrance

Woe! The wicked tricks they play
On a dark and drunken night
And the words owls may say
Bring on such a frozen fright
Before the blood boils
Back to its calmness
Beside the candle low
While the footsteps wound out faintly
Across the hardwood floors they know
When not a sack or a secret
Have wishes heard 'fore they must go

Hagan's Murder

Rough as a cob with more power than a hob
Changing the way of the old earth
It's the good and the bad
That makes the eyes sad
Having tears for salt and its worth
Now wind 'round the wise
To ponder the prize Given to the winner
Who waits in the glooms
To be told that his step
Should have crawled and then crept
Past the spirit then rising from tombs

Lèse Majesté

Untangle the tongues
Of the truest turned bad
Unravel the lungs
Of each breath that is sad
Move close toward the moment
Where never one my resist
The crowns that are shown
Upon the fingers of our fist

Hero, Cast Yourself into the Sea

With pirates in the port of doom
Craving about the treasures tomb
The parrot sings in bold brass cage
Pruning feathers from salt and age
He speaks:
"A bloody beak like mine has seen
Hard nights at sea no sailor's dream
Woe, wet, and dreary, swinging hard
Where the quills and ink of the bard
Spilt on the waves that had no shore
And not for these two witching wings
I'd be a sailor to the core."

We Suppose the Seeds Are Fast

An old bloody tale they cannot describe
Until the hand moves its space on air
With a silent look or hard, cold stare
Was first to rest in each chief's eye
When too far from over water
Any man came too close nearby

Know Ships of Salty Witches

With spirits writing in their log
They float across this bay in fog
An hourly mission
To find the verse that reigns
Over stupefactive skies
That fell they've seen all games
As the ink is known to take a mind
The arrow flies for the heart to find
Lines sunken in the flight of air
Which points us past the thought we share

Wolfing's House, Picturesque and Haunting

Weaves who work in toy suits of armor
In this Kaffir Land neighboring the charmer
Feel splendid his songs
Knowing best how to rally
Spun from old yarns
Learned out at sea in the galley
Though once on the loom
Or the proud paper to write
They flew through the memory
And left without sight

Sir Tiff or Cater to the Flow

The deepest sea, the bound brine
Shallow and wavy, waste their time
Speaking toward the sure shore that knows
Which way the sail most often blows
The mast and master wait the night
For pirate eyes that shine with blight
And ponder on the fools who fight
Over how they have lost their sight

Distant from Ears

Tying the end knot too far below
Back inside of the page0s
Breathing a spell past its glow
Growing thirsty for challenge
'neath the teeth cruelty bites
Where marble cities have stories
They whisper these nights

Brandish Your Claymore Perhaps

Saddle up, Bucephalus
His rider once was so great
Though he died at twenty-three
In a fit that called his fate
A general and a prince
All of history knows
Good this age that he had lived
From the plans that he once chose

Literature More Inspiring than Life

The crown of glory
The hunchback had found
So deep within Julia's eyes
Pods of whales with harpoon tales
Relate only through the guise
Brought up to hear
And quickly see the bell
Ringing on land
And far at sea as well

Beckon the Most Illustrious Animal Painter

Dealing with wild smugglers and bold brigands
Noble families find their safehold full.
The shepherd feels the breeze
And then he sees
His sheep are now shorn of their wool.
Winter brings the ice,
And no flames to save his herd.
While artists paint the prize
Above each written word.

Sinking Fleets of Warships

On this evil evening
Rogues run the moon too high
A sorry lot controls
The moving of the eye
There is murder in the making
A killing of the thought
Catching dreggish sword tips breaking
Into the master's plot

Knead the Dough

Ignite the fires of the imagination
Leave the faithful to their own frustration
Fuel the theories and the art of knowing
Until the Great Spirit is forever showing

The New and Enhanced Word Order

Logostic = word wisdom
Subjective non-necessities = People of no value
Versecopy = Denotation of evolutionary logostic abilities
Wivernous = An unbelievable chain of events
Memorative = Programmed recall
Neuropathobia = Human suffering
    caused by emotional rape

Chapter Two
The Sly Test Thought

And Drawn to Scale

Ours are knots needed
To tie time in a bow
Packaged in plain English
Are rhymes they chose to know
Few pin feathers please the falcons
Pluming on their bold breast.
Apart from the magic
Now building its own nest.
In the thicket of tricks
No wizards wish to test
Till the maps of travelers
Have been laid long to their rest

Five Spare Rows, Two Yards Deep

Dankly decks that dangle
Well over doom's dire glare
Where wild wont widows walk
And others never dare
Searching out the deprived
And their seafaring lives
Who left them most lonely
And wicked wanting wives

The Widow's Peak

Deep and far out, lost long before
The truth of sailing reaches its core
Man floats on his last stormy wave
Where vessels sank past knots that save
A sail falling, torn and weak
There mystery measure each peak

Drafts of the Ship Destroyed

Wreckage to reckon
Sunken and stray
Resting on bottom
Beneath each bay
Blisters on hands
From the anchor's rust
Sailing toward lands
With seaworthy lust

Beyond Bootlegs and Blood Feuds

The Brown Library, where is it now?
With volumes of Shakespeare wondering how
Left for the old dust unnoticed by man
Waiting for few with more humanly hand
To live on their page while under they stand
In cold blood and murder to take the command

Inside the Unknown Sea Krits

Poetry tears the air apart
And travels through the sailor's heart
Beating about the bows and sails
Beyond the books and all their tales
Past all the scorn with shadowed eyes
Above the suns, forever rise
Coiling questions sure to bite
At poisoned pages turned at night

Baffled the Beast of Them

These frozen chosen thoughts
Melting on the fire
Are turning to witans
Who wonder why they spire
For the strongest understanding
Of earth and all its ways
Is to rule each moment landing
At doors of every maze

Stern Galley Knot

Take platforms at your quarters
These waters weep of death
And no one has walked a plank
That now breathes or has a breath
The hidden gaff takes nothing
From the rising of the wave
Unless you count the fiendish fish
The captain has those to save

Like Wild Observers

Listening for the viewpoint
That never quite will be seen
While looking through the closed lids
Which lie sanded in their dream
We make the old proud decks
To fish for pretense and prawn
While caught up in the gold verse
In the name of its splay song
As buried firmans from the sultan
Escape the hands at shivering sea
Still on the land the lighthouse stands
Near where the family lives as free

'Neath the Sun Sculpture

The wind blows so many ways
It soon will once decide
Who has many attributes
We cannot set aside.
When each candle finds the light
The wicks will wonder why
Turning the most wicked flame
To burn within the sky.

Lowering the Gonfalon

Buck up, take heart
Ye morbid mind, the wind will start
Lo! To begin the blow
Read on and quickly find
The sails are bound
To know thy mind
These times are soon to beg and start
Beyond the ways of captain's heart
Whose ears heard each oar break
Before the breeze had blown
'way their worst and last mistake
No sailors were ever shown

Why, Sir, Come Speculate

Awe more often strays across the deck
Our lens not lost will not inspect
The sail far off miles on wavy sea
And tell for sure what its pencel be

Men Shun the Will

The deep pen dance of Poe
Dye verse with the meaning
As damp pens in the well
Reach writers' hands then tell.
The clay aims to be molded
And not cousin to the shore
Or any wild witches spell
That has not been cast before.

All About the End Counters

Which end of the wick shall burn tonight?
Upside down, the candle tricks the sight
'fore it takes its last quick wink
And starts to dream instead of think

A BREATHING SPELL

Flight Over Spanish Bayonets

Gyrfalcon fly through winds of cold
To ports where Spaniards savor gold
Slow your move with silver eye
You, they have not notice land or fly
The ice melts slow back at your home
As wings still wonder where you've flown
Your return may be someday
Though now your wish is here to stay

Seen from the Castles Bower

The bow of yew is strung and aimed
Arrow feathered and tip inflamed
The waxed and sized cord now proclaims
It will send shivers through their games

Ketch the Meaning

The howling pen hunts for thoughts to scribe
The captain stands it on its pointed end
To begin the log that's sure to bribe
The stingy queen for new sails and riggings
To fly above a freight of barreled rum
That he may nourish nightly
Before the light of dawn has come

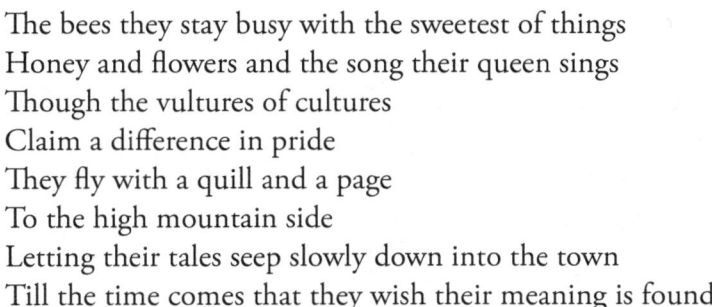

The Strength of One Wing

The bees they stay busy with the sweetest of things
Honey and flowers and the song their queen sings
Though the vultures of cultures
Claim a difference in pride
They fly with a quill and a page
To the high mountain side
Letting their tales seep slowly down into the town
Till the time comes that they wish their meaning is found

Mischievously Playing Perhaps

Inside the Marchen, our doing unfold the fall
From the Tarpeian cliff that is nothing at all.
The Rogues Galleries walls dare not ever hang our face
And the power to imagine we stretch and erase.
Inside the mind we travel completely unknown
To the owners of thoughts who are more often prone
To never believe or thoroughly know
How far our power can constantly go.

To Display Our Own Magic

Druidical druthers, thy cave be so clean
Your wizard works hard to not ever been seen
Moving the novels to remove their dust
And wiping the shelves more free of their lust
He cudgels the brain
Till the answer lies perfectly bare
In the drolleries chapter
That describes why we care

Sheltered Shady Sorcerers

Cross swords with the incantations
Near the currents of their creation
Then watch the effigies burn in spite
Hung in the breeze to move the light
Shadows follow as fast as sight
To catch them chasing objects
With all their might

The Gift of Simile

Plagiarizes of the epic wish to design as sweet
The short and simple meanings
That feel themselves complete
The brush of most all paintings
Learns how the colors blend
'fore the scene is noticed
Giving flowers to its friend

Deeper in the Spell

My magic limbs will reach forever
Around the fields and minds so clever
The fox will spread with wildest of hare
Below the wings of hawks where you now stare
At last you walk upon the finest floor
A beings thoughts might ever once explore

Unto Us That Is

Members of the peerage
Now stare through the knights last thoughts
To leave the castle lonely
And cut the bridges knots.
"Hindering the passage
Of our foe and friends alike
Would damage so severely
The calmness of our psych.
With him we must do something
To change his evil scheme.
Call the court magician now
To put him in a dream
That we may speak then softly
Into his slumbered mind
To suggest that he never do anything unkind."

Below Two Wings

Over dew the falcon does fly
Its wings will hew the air and eyes
Its beak bows proudly toward its prey
That runs for cover in bales of hay
Into mist our minds are quickly lead
When we realize the shrew has fled

The customary host of telepathic nations sees the infancy of its global veil daily being lifted uncertainly, with numbers cushioning the obscure and difficult conclusions that the absolute are purely guided through thought formats that have succeeded and paralleled themselves in any obvious fashion respectful to the gift of communication. More than any other moment. Two minds in conversation. Able to exchange ideas past any other previous social intercourse in life.

For those unfamiliar with the gift, we wonder what it is their minds project for the future?

Golden Isis Magazine
Gerina Dunwich, Editor
PO Box 726
Salem, Massachusetts 01970

Reviewed by Gerina Dunwich

Hour of De Wolf A Collection of Poems by Fletcher DeWolf (hardcover, 122 pages, no illustrations), Vantage Press, NY 1988. This book is an absolute must for all lovers of good poetry: *Hour of De Wolf,*

written by a very talented New England poet and musician whose work also appears in *Golden Isis Magazine*, is a poetic odyssey through an array of stimulating images. I thoroughly enjoyed this book and found much of the rhymed poetry in it to be quite exceptional and filled with meaning. Though I would not consider this a Wiccan book, there were a few poems with occult themes ("Castle of Necromancy," "Benevolent," "Palm Reader"), and these, of course, were my favorites.

Elven Glen Maven-Mentioned

The rural lass, she is so fine
Her sheep's eye always catches mine
The sheaves of stocks across the life
Are bound much as our minds belief
The haulm we find at harvest end
Helps to make shawms with which we send
A tune whose notes the wind will often hold
To weave inside the heart that's feeling old

Alive to the Danger

Our verses are fledged to take on heights
Read in the darkness of foggy nights
Outside the yard where spirits rise
From the kist of long passed away
With eyes that blink upon their prey

Deadly Nightshade

This dungeon doth not raze thy thought
Outside the eye perceives their knot.
"Tis tied tight for thine very own
Once highly worshipped lord on throne.
His rule is musty, and webs grow wide
To haunt each vein beneath his hide.
A call for aid will not be reckoned
By those so strongly he has beckoned,
For they know the court magician more than well
Is one of power with no suspicious spell.
Each is pure and placed precisely right
As the words they read here on this night.

We Are the Versed Ones to Know

Are these words from a wonder
A war in the mind
With a meaning that no one
On earth could once find?
Never so hard have the eyes tried to see
The source of their being pure sorcery
Surely a secret is something
We all think we must know
Though without the thought of another
It will never be so

Listen My Children   May 90 Issue
Free Copy

A Dualistic Mind

When I see the design
Of your thought
I remember the memories
That you forgot
Holding on to the flower
Of spring
We both will remember
Everything

Sit in your favorite chair and just relax, or sit under a tree
and rest. For the hour of DeWolf is upon you.

Peregrine the Poet

He knows the verses of the Vikings
And sharpens every sorcerers' sword
While he keeps the lightning striking
Upon the minds that would be bored

Ewer Pouring the Wine

During the flagrante delicto scribing
The pens anger becomes more inflamed
For the fact that its master may never be tamed
"Please write of beautiful peace
And the kindness of mankind
Through darkness so blind
May I never have the pleasure
Of one sympathetic day
When you use me
For lovely poetic passion and play?"

The Webs of William

The quills of his cleverness fly by in our mind
with the deepest of meaning we often can find
ourselves caught in his mire to quickly appear
entangled by the quotes of William Shakespeare.

Peer Amid the Riddles

The Wiccals thicker in the morning hour
When we wake from our dream
With a greater power
And the magic is mild by the time of noon
Waiting for the knight to tell spells
That have come from his tomb

Moon Deems Our Destiny

Cockcrows break us from our spell as we hear the tolling knell; now another, no longer here dwells. Tonight's moon will watch his spirit rise; no tears will shed from its golden eyes, for long before the time of man, it was placed high to understand that the ways inside our mind so fine often change below its yellow shine.

Preying Closely

Gypsies warning the stars in the sky; the falcons
Have flown on farther by, leaving their nest without
A note to find the quill with which the poet wrote.

POETRY SPACE

Tracts for the Times

The verse that holds the sword of Damocles
Has secrets in its sheath
Time whisper to the willows
That wizards work high and low beneath
The common thoughts and wayward wishes
Cast upon each star
That claim the skies have collected them
To carry us a far
To gather in the forest
Then look for open trails
To travel to the towns
And spread out timbered tales

Evening Rays

Lo! Great blue heron wade the marsh
The sound of hunters fades less harsh
Water ripples with fewer fears
In silent sets the sun appears
Atop the hills strong green shoulder
To realize your wings have grown older

For the Catalysis of Tragedy

Awe ties the mist to dry winds
Taken from fields of visions
Claws sink into the flies wing
Cast in its baited mission
The angler hears the cat's cry
With bleeding paw on barb of hook
Curious he catches both eyes
Upon the wound that has them look

Talons and Tail Rhyme

Birds that have the power to calm the raging sea
Share their wings with poets on shores
    where winds blow free
Loyal to their flight both have tamed the rack of waves
That flood our minds at night
With dreams the spirit saves.

It's Not the Lift, It's the Sort

Bows jest atop the presents
They pleasantly adorn.
The papers beneath their knots
Will soon be cast and torn.
The girt it might be mammoth
Or of the small variety,
But in the thought of giving
Is where receivers' eyes should see.

Melodies of Magic

The time has set the tune, the notes they never mind
Playing to the ears, both wicked and most kind
The owl he seldom wanders from his perch at night
Although it seems to us at times he surely might
His wisdom is profound and needs not question who
For all the thoughts we have, he clearly sees on through
He turns his head away, then points out
with his feathered wing
Where he will fly and sing

Building the Meaning

The hew man eyes after cutting blows
Is to the line the chisel knows
No need for hammers or beveled blade
The form is perfect the axe has made.

Lore in the Way of Morgan Le Fay

I work in spells the morning tells its flower
Some be good and some be quite bad
This life is such that we must dab
A little and a lot each way
And those with eyes who come and rise
Upon our hills and unmade bed
Have been overheard by ones who sigh
And simply say
These words we wish were never said
Nor written in this way

Faustian Feathers

'Tis told wizards work in rime
Leaving scenes on windows in the cold,
and their source of sorcery
is worth more than stars of solid gold.
If one should call your name
or walk within your dream,
let doubters die in sham
for he they've never seen.
Perhaps he has come from Tartarus
or the skies of way beyond;
though for sure each day we'll listen
and hear his message grow more strong.

Lusus Naturae

This life lacks the shine illusion gives
when asleep in dream the hero lives
constant cries crowd the dawn
even fowl carry on.
Let's take each moment the mystery leaves
and pass it on to whoever disbelieves,
then wonder will beset their mind
and more in life they'll start to find.
To hear rows of reddish princes feather
discuss the clouds and the changing weather
then listen close for the knight in gale;
the winds will whisper soft of his tale
though tell not a soul what the tall oak does know,
its limbs will sway with secrets
that always grow.

Brilliant Qualities

The tall coven tree shades at times
The witch who's best at working rhymes
Beneath its limbs, she weaves the cape
for winters winds that will come late.
The seasons know her hands not cruel
that form the growth of Nature's pool,
though many never sight her ways
and have not thought what fills her days.
She still maintains the garden's glory
tells best of all what's in her story.

Peer Amid the Riddles

The Wicca is thicker in the morning hour
when we wake from our dream
with a greater power.
The magic is milder by the time of noon
waiting for the knight to tell spells
that have come from his tomb.
Sir Roger de Coverley
is the dance we shall do
till the music is over
and the evening too.

Gifted Voices

On your finger I wish to place
this ominous magical ring
for with it you'll rule the sky and land
with the slightest move of your hand
'twas for sure there are not of thee
and it be hunted by many
with this you must move through the night
scribe the verse that is most right
for ones to learn
how things of the future will be
when first their eyes sights
sure the lore of sorcery

On Second Thought

The tailor has come to the bakery mart
hearing angry words from the owner's heart.
"Practice your lies and your grave mistruth,
the last thing they'll feel is the edge of your tooth."
"Why such advice have you given to a cobbler's son?
Who has sunk every nail on the very sole that you run."
"He has stolen my cakes from the bakery shelf
and acts with the mischief of the green forest elf."
"Perhaps he was hungry and you nowhere to be found,
Or back near the oven rising you dough by the pound."
"I did leave with my door open
for some afternoon rays,
and perhaps I am mistake for where my blame quickly lays.
I see that there's money 'neath the mat of my vault,
And wrong have I done to place the bitter fault."

Decided Inside the Donjon

As merlons and crenels line the walls
The knight of another kingship calls
"Inside your realm, near to the helm
have you one who writes?
Our shield and our sword have lost their lord
and win no more our fights.
'Tis from your barrister we sense this spell
that a quill has written and not wished us well.
Its ink we feel is blood most real
from the dragon that lured the mist
near our fields and tower light
each thirteenth hour and seventh night
to fright us from its way
and most of all we wonder tall
if for your scop you did slay
to fill his well, to write the spell
that covers us this day."

Forever

The labors of the line and the magic of the verse
twinkle on the vine that the witches use to curse
Those who fall behind and believe its superstition
are most likely not to find
that first was built the place perdition.
Good and bad are real and as simple as the light
though to not know them both is the worst oversight
I hear this from the cave where Merlin beckons me
to work the wizard's lave and write their poetry.

From Under the Staff A shepherd and his dog

Rest the night away
While the flock it slowly moves
through the meadow and its hay
the morning waits its own
time and place to be
when no longer may the twain
keep from the land that's free.

A COLLECTION OF POEMS

Guinevere's Wish for Warriors

Broadswords slash the armor
While spears sing through the skies
From behind the shield a charmer
Has looked with penetrating eyes

"This battle must be over
for all of the deceased
Let's stand here in the clover
and become more man than beast"

About Beauty

Count her balance to be forceful
her vision with the finest edge
and her wishes trimmed more neatly
than hawthorns in their glossy hedge.
Her glance that gathers all
keeps kings upon their toes
and tells the core of magic
everything it ever knows.

The Bitter Flight

Chuck Will's widow at the feeder finds
Power winds with snow that blinds over tree
Tops to where the village sets she flies for thee
Of the baker's pets cold old loaves of bread
Most stale but good greet her beak to cease
The hungers hood, her wings near froze before
She did arrive though then had been chose to surely
survive

To Comprehend

The ways of the witches are today
More well-known
than in earlier times
when their power was show.
The wizard and the wand
they both know too
the great spirit rules inside me and you
we are surely together here on this earth
to make magic appear for all of its worth
though those with the doldrums
and the lingering lie
wish most for our finish
and the day we will die.
Fools on the corner and the near thorough fare
still have no answers they may ever compare
bound into the spirit we travel on by
with mysterious herbs
the world must soon try.

My Parents

All of us have two
That we feel close and love
But my two are most special
And I feel far above
If words could come out
And clearly once say
How deeply I feel
For their God-given way
Then let them be right now
Here in this verse
With no feelings
We ever will need to rehearse

The Mind's Mirror

This day has dwindled before my eyes
It's castle stands, row with no surprise
Alone and misty in its fog set spell
Its empty throne has one rule left to tell.

Once there was the sorcerer fair
Who wrote the words that few did share.
A secret magic kept the flame
Burning beneath his hidden name.
On scroll with ink and feathered quill
He designed the kingdoms only will
To seek the secret of the last unknown
And find the place where magic's always shown.

The Beginning

Lay bare the deepest bold thought
The origin of evil
And how it's never been caught
Then open the gate wide
For the gold hinge will melt
Forming the ring for the hand
That has never felt

The Real Flow of Blood

Blindfolded horses in the bull's way
Slaughtered by horns of the distant prey
Many are the gores that drop in agony
For the spectators eyes that wait to see

From the Flames

They will leave us lonely
To pick up our mind
From the gutter and grave
No others could find
They will put out the mat
And welcome the host
whose left his last wish
With an unfriendly ghost
They never will need us
To clean their old throne
For now we have flown clear
And designed our own

Dearest Vivian

Lady of the lake, she walks before me
Controlling each image I happen to see
Vibrant her wish that the magic may spin
Our minds further out and deeper within
Her veil and her dress both flow to command
That the book that she holds all must understand
Pages with spells and others with prayers
Or so they're defined by our minds many layers

One, Two, Three

Words will not describe
When death's prescribed
And placed upon the door
To lift the mat and tip the hat
Above the head that counts the score

With Poetic Sorcery

None with an eye or open mind to land near
May ever dispute that the power is clear
Above and beyond and beneath our last touch
Comes the fear that our thoughts
Have grown far too much

The First Year In Class

Of mean scholarship
and an eye for the worst
thinking and knowing
the thought that was first
writing the rhymes
that most men would hang
is part of the song
the beggars one sang

Resting Up For The Ride

Death round the corner
Pointing the way
Off the tombstone
Whose verse seems to say
Beneath this soil
I will rest in the sun
"Til my night sets
And my spirit shall run
Deep into the city,
Then far from its smog
To ride slowly by
Each still pond below fog
Then back in the dawn
To the most secretive plot
To where never my spirit
May ever be caught

Waiting One Minute

The guide to the ball
Sees gowns near the floor
On his ride to the hall
Where he's not been before.
The dance soon starts
To take hearts and their beat
More serious than ever
One dares to repeat

Presentation Of The Character

The goldsmith's chisel
has employed the shrewd shape
now cast and sewn into the sorcerer's cape.
Designs are from the mystery of myth
as the points on our star count to the fifth.
His words are selected to signal the start
of magic and mirth found quickly out the play
we all have been chosen to act in this day.

A Dualistic Mind

When I see the design of your thought
I remember the memories that you forgot
holding onto the flower of spring
we both will remember everything

From One Cloud To Another

Wariest Dis describes the mist
That sets the world today
The clouds grow dark
And wait the spark
To spread their bolts of prey
The mind snaps a shot
At what its thought
As light cast wide its warn
Then awe quickly spreads
Throughout the heads
That sees the skies sharp scorn

Preying Closely

Gypsies warning the stars in the sky
the falcons have flown on further by
to find the quill
with which the poet wrote.

Gifted Voices

On your finger I wish to place
This ominous magical ring
For with it you'll rule the sky and land
With the slightest move of your hand
'Twas for sure there are not of thee
And it be hunted by many
With this you must move through the night
And scribe the verse that is most right
For ones to learn
How things of the future will be
When first their eyes sight
Sure the lore of sorcery

Night Owl

The levels of our thoughts are made
by mirrors and the myths that fade
from the lines the poets keep
in their minds
when fast asleep
a curse of sin
and lies will tell
of ideas gone deeper than the well
secrets on the lips of man
cannot be heard to understand
a power past the flesh and blood
has turned the soil with rain to mud
now past the point
where all have seen writes on a wizard
with a dream
to tell the world
it's met its might
as it's now turning day to night

One Rhetorical Question

The court magician jumps and swims the moat
while the jester reads what the queen last wrote
bring me the power and bring me it fast
the spells of witches that forever last
that I may place them on the head
of everyone who has not read
the words of Merlin here on this mortal day
that change our minds in the most distinctive way

The Mind's Mirror

This day has dwindled before my eyes
Its castle stands, now with no surprise
Alone and misty in its fog set spell
Its empty throne has one rule left to tell.
"Once there was the sorcerer fair
Who wrote the words that few did share.
A secret magic kept the flame
Burning beneath his hidden name.
On scroll with ink and feathered quill
He designed the kingdom's only will
To seek the secret of the last unknown
And find the place where magic's always shown."

The Webs Of William

The quills of his cleverness fly by in our mind
With the deepest of meaning we often can find
Ourselves caught in his mire to quickly appear
entangled by the quotes of William Shakespeare.

To The Lands Of Forgotten Magic

Seeing into and knowing of
what goes beyond this hate and love
what designs are left
when minds go far to the sky
out past each place
that's known to the familiar eye
then back inside the candle clear
that lights each step to disappear
beneath the feet who know below
is where each soul always go!

The Poetic Temperament

Pursuing graceless sinners
Through the old alehouse door
Their rudeness in spirit has given before
Professors of thetoric their bitter core
From the rising glow and inner life of man
Near sleepy hollow now their stolen command

The Tartarean Future

Tears today and long tomorrows
flooding into ponds of sorrows
gray gowns on the marble floor
wipe the footprints furthermore
from the walk and pathway clean
'fore the eyes have clearly seen.

With Our Own Two Eyes

Clever conclusions creep
from behind the dark door
then speak to the silence.
Woe! Lord must there be more
knights they have sat
and thought through the mist
of queen's they never wished to resist
all it has trouble though
will soon solve its own plight
as we read the magic moonlight.

Overlooking Food for Thought

Dumbness and numbness,
who knows all of the most?
Is it not the spirit
who dines with its ghost?
Or is it the traveler
on top of each hellion hill,
staring down on the widow,
rewriting her husband's last will?

"This world's mind is, for the most part, biblically and
politically brainwashed. A far more finer earth it would be
if its mind was more poetically potent."

We are the Versed Ones to Know

Are these words from a wonder
A war in the mind
With a meaning that no one
On earth may once find?
Never so hard have the eyes tried to see
The source of their being pure sorcery.
Surely a secret is something
We all think we must know
Thought without the thought of another
It will never be so.

The Disembodied Spirit of Robin Goodfellow

The leaves partly for rest
Cushion the feet of wee sprite
The moon on the field has shadows at night
Where we dance with ink
From the blue- and blackberry he fills
The thoughts that we read and we think
"Til the winter air comes and it chills
We will play through the end of each fall
To design the most cheerful times of them all.

Ride On

The summer shines in your eyes
bring the lakes their own surprise
chain and spokes with all those folks
sitting round the fire they're burning
let us know when you stop learning.

The Castalian Crave

Let's weave a spell this wondrous night
Beneath the willows and steeple's light
Let's move our chariot to another stall
Where steeds and stallions wait for us to call
Far above the heads of shepherd's sheep
Where all good secrets seem best to keep.

My Parent's

All of us have two that we feel close and love
Though my two are most special and I feel far above
If words could come out and clearly once say
How deeply 1 feel for their God given way
Then let them be here right now in this verse
With no feelings we over will need to rehearse.

A COLLECTION OF POEMS

Guinevere's Wish for Warriors

Broadswords slash the armor
While spears sing through the skies
From behind the shield a charmer
Has looked with penetrating eyes

"This battle must be over
For all of the deceased
Let's stand here in the clover
And become more man than beast."

A Majestic Stroll

The hem is sphering round her shawl
She leads him through the forest tall
with whispers that are seasoned well
and secrets he could never tell
please do stop here but for a while
to wait the sun and its bright smile
the magic spun beneath this tree
with roots of charm and sorcery
I am Lady Fay you've heard them say
and sister to the ruling king
on your finger I wish to place
the magical ominous ring

The Timeless Vinegrowers

The shade hears the wind
The door feels the hand
The roses they speak
That the thorns understand
Taking life from the earth
Before it has time
To show more of its worth
With the sorcerer's rhyme.

In A Fair Way

Trusty sword to slice away
The last of verse on lips to say
Sparks of joy, wonder, lust
Read into the poem
Just what they must
No eye has ever known no sleep
Or seen a secret not to keep
Like legend links its fingers well
Around what never one must tell
How lot or little they might know
Is nothing more than what they show

Waking with Elf Locks

Cicerone surely is tired today
He's caught a spell from the forest day
Too deeply into and through the magic limbs
He'd taken his seers to suit the elf's whims
"No crowd comes near to my tree trunk
Spreading their noise and useless junk
If I've told him once it now rears twenty-eight
That there's nothing on earth wore that I hate
Then to hear the roaring and the branches break
Perhaps this sleep shall do him some greater good
As he dreams-I'll move his thoughts as they should
Not to be a bother and come roaming near
My forest home or my growing garden dear."

Laughing Stalks The Quod

Cunningly sought and sifted through crafty screens
Nightmares and adventure are built in our dreams
Clouds set on the castle spreading deeply their midst
While inside his chamber the king pounds his fist.
"Where is the magician? I cannot sleep come the dark
I need a potion, a spell, or a charm to embark
One of three he must give quickly to me
To put an end to this restless insanity."
The jester eavesdrops and steps quietly inside
Offering help with his humblest of pride.
As he quizzes fast, he did hear him say,
"I've noticed you nap in the middle of the day-"
"I see that your fear has caused you to lie
And twice more the worse on me you did spy."
"I am sorry, my lord, curiousness had me caught,
And it is for you only I wish sleep of the sort."
"Go to tell your jokes in the dungeon dire squire,
For you've set my content rear the angry fire."
He's off to the dungeon with an escort or two
Down in the cellar with his sorrow he will stew.
"Damn this cold doom and curse his old crown
He has more spite than any I've found."
Then near his door locked doubly tight
Through a small window he sees the light.
"I have the key to set you and your humor free,
And the wizard of all quods I certainly be.
I know this be hard, though clear I have spoke
'fore I turn the lock, I must hear a joke."
"It's no laughing matter, me in this dire hole,
And you want to hear humor, such a curious soul."
"Well, my dear friend, is it not certainly true
For the same reason you have been placed here too?"
"Aye, that it is and now I shall tell
The joke that will free me from this cell.
There once was a cobbler who nailed his own sole
To the floor of his kitchen to take a long stroll."
"Ah, funny you are, and laugh I have done
Now walk out this door, and fast may you run."

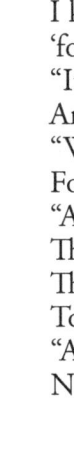

Shades of Glow

Moods are made of many tones
Loops and squares of hollow bones
Broken by another chill
Written in a center's will
Deep inside a marble desk
With draws of jade and alabaster
Paper marked to read and fill
Thought that's born just to kill
Living in an old grist mill
With webs of air where rooms are full
With words that stop and start to pull
The mind make simple task, they say
Working on the world each day
Its mood of matter, myth, and match
Controlled to think that it must catch
The words and verse permissible
Challenging the mark of time
Or who has made this roulette line?
A graze that we call fine
Ending in the field of night
A dream has stayed to call what's right.

"For sure an uphill climb, writing plus publishing poetry demands a love for its power. It must, and does, stand alone as the world's pleasing form of communication, although many go through life without ever having its blossom unfold upon them. Be that as it may, posts and poetry readers are increasing in numbers and awareness of its importance. My personal approach to the art has developed in the form of creating puzzles with words, hopefully triggering thought."

More Sew Than Knot, My Dear Persephone

Lo! She still be there unto this day
The gown she wears has mortals sway
The sound she layers into our play
With harps tuned to the earth
Her pluck is wild and twice her child
That's grown into the finest of all sage
To scribe the night with verses bright
Beyond any bard on page.

Die Just Before The Meal

How deep in the heart must the steel blade sink
Before the mind has stopped to slowly think
Where will the last link find the hidden hasp
While contemplating it must surely ask
The necklace turning from gold to gray
On throats that swallow each word we say.

Weighty In Matter

Periods of calm follow outrage
Given to reason found on the page
Books have their battle
To conquer the eye
But better the mind
To be their next try.

Formation

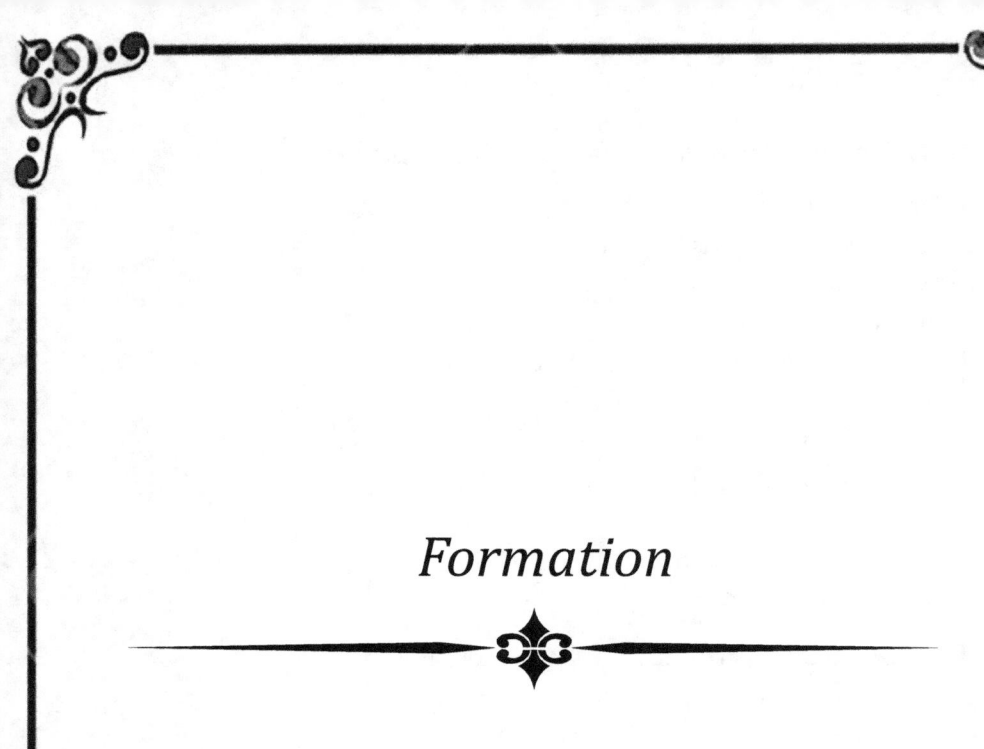

A COLLECTION OF POEMS

An entree of parnassian and samothracian entelechics both cloud and clear the sky of the mind. Our neurological cameras will hopefully take numerous snapshots to later be developed inside the subconscious dark rooms, for future observance in our consciousness, as we awake and read again.

Here the curtain closes only to be reopened for the Black Ace and those of World War Two, namely of barracks 36B of STAGLAG 17B, who contributed to "The Ballard of Bold Stud Bill," "Staglag Highlights," "Draftdodger."

The Ballad Of Bolt Stud Bill

There are some who say that a gunners
    pay is altogether too high,
But that ain't so because we all know,
    we earn it when we fly.

It's a rugged game, and there ain't much
    fame, and life at its best is short,
For the men who dare to fight in the air
    for the silver wings they sport.

Now I'm going to tell a tale of hell, of guts and iron will,
Of the war in the sky by the men who fly, and
    the twenty-fifth mission of Bolt Stud Bill.

Now Bill was one of those gambling guys;
    he harbored a lust for the game.
Cards, dice, roulette, or just any damn
    bet, to Bill it was all the same.

He couldn't tame his lust for the game,
    and he'd sit in every night,
He'd get his pay and then he'd play until
    time for the morning flight.

If you couldn't find Bill dealing blackjack or stud,
    and in the barracks he couldn't be seen,
he'd be crouched by his guns dealing death
    to the Huns from the tail of a B-17.

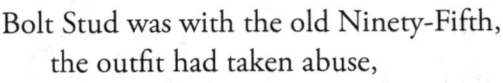

Bolt Stud was with the old Ninety-Fifth,
　　the outfit had taken abuse,
For each raid we'd made to "Jerry" we paid,
　　the price of a couple of crews.

Then into the group replacements would
　　troupe, eager for missions to face.
They would make just a few, and then a new
　　crew would fly in and take their place.

It got pretty rough, and a bunch of the lads
　　were discussing the problem one night,
While passing round the bottle they found
　　and proceeding to get kind of tight.

One of the guys considered quite wise,
　　a mathematical "Slick,"
With paper and pen, and a drink now and
　　then, promised the problem he'd lick.

With glasses of scotch, they sat round and
　　watched an anxious blurry-eyed lot.
Slick sweat and he swore and cursed the air
　　corps, until finally this answer he got.

"I've figured it out, and there isn't a doubt,
　　no matter how hard you strive.
I'm willing to bet there's none who will get
　　through mission number twenty-five."

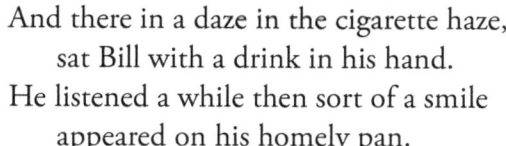

And there in a daze in the cigarette haze,
    sat Bill with a drink in his hand.
He listened a while then sort of a smile
    appeared on his homely pan.

Slick liked to choke on the words that Bill
    spoke, and the room went suddenly still.
"I've got a hunch there's one in the bunch,
    so I'll take that bet," said Bill.

"I'll tell you what, we'll make a pot,
    so come on, boys, chip in.
I'm willing to bet on my gambler's luck
    that I am the guy who'll win."

There is no mistake the odds were great,
    but the lure of chance is strong,
So one by one into the pot they flung their
    dough, and the game of chance was on.

It was early spring when they started the thing
    and when summer had rolled around.
Left of the men there were only ten,
    the rest were all shot down.

Bill always thought of the bet they made
    and cursed that fatal night,
And he'd sometimes say in a troubled way,
    "It looks like Slick was right."

But still he flew, though well he knew,
    the fickleness of fate,
Then he'd think of the dough and off he'd
    go, and another raid he'd make.

He squawked and moaned in a dreary tone
    and swore he would fly no more,
and in this way, he found one day, that
    he'd finished twenty-four.

But the combat game demands a price
    that all must pay who fly.
This settled fate, you can't escape,
    and pay you must or die.

For such is the law of the ETO; there's
    no exceptions to the rule,
    And so it was with Bill he'd been through
    the mill; he'd paid his debt in full.

His weight was down to a hundred pounds;
    he walked like a man in a daze.
He had a blank sort of look, and his hand, it
    shook; he had changed in many ways.

He had the purple heart and the DF,
    air medal with clusters four,
For Bill had made twenty-four raids,
    and he'd only to go one more.

He was sweating out this one more trip,
    holding out for an easy one,
and there happened by chance a raid to France
    that looked like an old milk run.

The briefing was done, and the morning
    sun was just coming up in the east.
They cleared the props and pulled the
    chocks and took off for La Pallice,

Bill in the tail watched the vapor trails,
    as over the channel they flew,
And he thought of the bet and the dough he'd
    get when his last mission was through.

They carried a sight on this flight for
    they were leading the way.
As the hours passed, they came at last
    to where the target lay.

With anxious eyes, he searched the sky,
    no fighters could he see,
but the sky was black with bursting flack
    as they reached the old I.P.

Then they swung on the bombing run;
    their course was level and true.
They were flying by the PDI as the target came in view.

Bill's brow was wet with clammy sweat as
    they opened the big bomb bay.

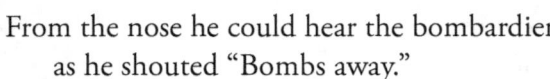

From the nose he could hear the bombardier
    as he shouted "Bombs away."

Bill glanced at his watch and he said with a
    grin, "We'll hit the target at noon,
and this is the easiest raid we've ever made,"
    but he spoke a little too soon.

For his ship gave a lunge in a downward
    plunge, like a barge on a heavy sea.
"Well, I guess this is it, we've sure been hit,
    and it looks pretty bad to me."

And to his dismay when the smoke cleared away,
    Bill saw that two engines were out,
Then from the waist, a tone of haste,
    he heard a gunner shout.

"Get set for trouble 'cause we're falling behind,
    and there's fighters coming in fast."
Right then and there, Bill breathed a prayer,
    as the first Folke Wolf flashed past.
He tightened his grip and bit his lip,
    and settled down to fight.
His shoulders slouched in a gunner's
    crouch behind his optical sight.

The big guns bounced and bucked in their
    mounts, spewed forth their laden death,
As he swung his gun on the diving Hun
    that was coming in fast on his left.

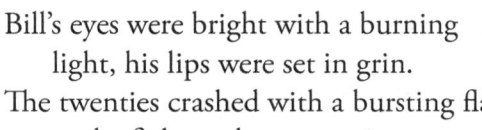

Bill's eyes were bright with a burning
    light, his lips were set in grin.
The twenties crashed with a bursting flash
    as the fighter plane came in.

In streaks of red the tracers sped, Bill
    knew his aim was right,
For the Jerry plane, in a burst of flame,
    blew up within his sight.

Through burst of flack and fighter attack,
    the big ship staggered on,
Still in control, though shot full of holes,
    and two of the engines gone.

Up in the front the pilot was slumped,
    three bullets through his head.
In the waist of the ship with a shattered hip,
    lay one gunner dying, the other dead.

Shot in the shoulder and half in hell, Bill
    crouched in a bloody spray.
"I've lost the bet, but I am not licked yet, come
    on, you Hinies, and get your pay."

In they came with guns aflame, like
    hornets from their nest,
And, well, Bill knew by the way they flew
    they were Hermann Göring's best.

Through the tracers flash and cannons
    crash, he heard the copilot shout
In a crackling tone on the interphone
    the order to bail out.

Bill saw at a glance they hadn't a chance;
    his luck had passed him by,
for their gallant plane was a coffin of
    flame; it was hit the silk or die.

The engineer and the bombardier were
    first to use their chutes,
and the rest of the crew that was able
    to all quickly followed suit.

Out of the sky in a screaming dive, the
    Jerry swooped in for the kill,
and hating to quit though he knew he was
    licked, the last to leave was Bill.

Out Bill came from the burning plane,
    like a human zephyr on high.
He grabbed for his ring and got the thing, and
    plunged downward through the sky.

When your life depends on odds and
    ends, of silk and cords and such,
right then and there Bill breathed a prayer,
    'cause his life wasn't worth very much.

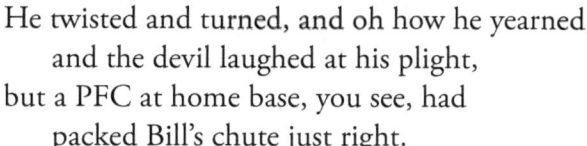

He twisted and turned, and oh how he yearned,
    and the devil laughed at his plight,
but a PFC at home base, you see, had
    packed Bill's chute just right.

With a tug on his back, up went the slack,
    and his parachute started to sway.
He glanced all around but heard not a sound,
    for the planes had flown on their way.

And below him lay the Bay of Biscay; he
    knew he'd be in for a swim.
There, broad, bleak, and black, with little white
    caps, the water rushed up to him.

Bill had lost his bet and had many regrets, for
    the French coast was far out of view,
And England's shore he'd see no more;
    his life was just about through.

Bill should have quit like his old pal Slick,
    then he'd be safe at home.
Bill drowned that day in the black cold bay;
    he went underneath the foam.

Men can't understand that when fate takes a
    hand, the odds against them are great,
Bill was in trouble, and down for a double, and
    now his luck had drawn him an ace.

Now if there's still some who say that a
    gunner's pay is altogether too high
Well, just think of old Bill and his iron
    will and his last battle in the sky.

Stalag Highlights

Thirteen barracks in a row,
three thousand men sleep head to toe.
Plywood and boards make a bed,
rolled-up tunic to hold your head.
Two little blankets hold out the cold,
hundreds of lice hide in each fold.
Dirty latrines that stink of lime,
walls that are made of mud and slime.
Food served us in a dirty pail,
bread that moldy, hard, and stale.
Stoves that have no fuel to burn,
dirt that makes your stomach turn.
Jerry guards that patrol each fence.
always alert and on the defense.
This is the life an airman will see
when he hits the silk over Germany.

Draftdodger

I'm writing this short letter, and every word is true.
Don't look away, "DRAFTDODGER,"
    for it's addressed to you.
You feel at ease and in no danger, back
    in the old hometown.
You cook up some pitiful story so the
    draft board will turn you down.
You never think of real men who leave home day by day;
You think only of their girlfriends that
    you take while they're away.
You sit at home and read your paper, you
    jump and yell, "We'll win."
Just where do you get that we stuff this
    war will be won by men?
Just what do you think "DRAFTDODGER,"
    what this free nation would do?
If all the men were slackers and afraid to fight like you.
Well, I guess that's all, Mr. Slacker, I
    suppose your face is red.
America is no place for your kind, and
    I mean every word I've said.
So I'm closing this, "DRAFTDODGER,"
    just remember what I say,
Just keep away from my girl for I'm
    coming home someday.

Hg's War Of The Words

1. "You could not write your way out of a wet paper bag," wrote the bard unto the scop. "Grand illusions stand round you as you think you're at the top."

2. "Such kind words, my fellow pen, placed in your hand to verse. Read on, my distant friend, for times have not been worse."

1. "The events have held no meaning while all dates did not exist, unless you think you've more to make the mind's first written twist."

2. "Why filter me for feeling, when you say I see the ceiling through a mirror called the top?"

1. "Two fools they always find their way out of the dark, unless a third may lead them, past the poetic spark."

2. "Are you not one yourself, asking for another to toss in his talent or his thought of where this did begin?".

1. "Was first 1 who spoke to damn your foolish style, might you wonder more whose start has made this dawn designed with guile?"

2. "No talk of the makers makes more sense to me, than all your rigid rimes, written clear to see."

1. "My words, I do not claim, nor say they may be mine, while yours you keep to name though never raise to once supine."

2. "Enough! Now I surrender, submitting to my sleep. Although this woe of ours, I shall forever keep." Was first I who spoke to damn you foolish style.

Nowhere But Up

Out of any league, in form of interpretation, where the
    sharpest eye won't see how clear the observation.
Pathic past the point of version or any deep impress.
A Sphinx of subtle sound, no one has heard,
    to call themselves to higher ground.
Not aorist or fusty, nor futual floating fire, each moment
    meets us mending the ways in which we spire.

Small Change

Four openers, the safe says it does own its mind that is made up clearly, to not take off its gown that its insides may spread freely across the sleeping town.

Its feelings, they are none, though thoughts are many flown above the likes of some, who would like to take it home.

"Why, inside may be empty hot air to host your likes, no nails of hate an envy standing tall at spikes.

Recall, I'm only placed here to hold the gold and wine, one thought that he had drank and spent before the end of time.

Then silver slips its voice, inside the verse and tale, to tell it too may never feel one's quickly kettledrummed timbale.

"Perhaps a taste would treat you kindly, more pleasant than a touch," mumbles diamonds from their ring, on the hand that owns to much

"Never mind your mappings, they interest none my style. I'm off to search the village, forever waiting trial. The one held for the openers, four count their heads maybe though sooner than they think, permutation might they see."

Nature Inside the Castle

On a back road headed toward the meaning are passing thoughts of churches with their steeples leaning.

Damn those dirty couplets, repeating every time; now the choir has studied to sing their different rhyme.

Sense peaks round the corner, posing a sike, he riles the hills for heckling, then claims Helen to be his wife.

Personified, the picture still hangs there on the wall, claiming its the English scholar who knows the most of all.

About Jobs Pottery

Imagery at best, my cloche, with all its many names, sells there in the market where wide eyes chase the mind that never tames.

How fat it has grown in its old unruly age; perhaps it's made to think once on each seventh night.

What page has come with thunder and told the world to write.

School Maid

Playing primero with poetry, each poem a
    card itself, shuffled 'neath the novice
    whose pen plays to the shelf.
Near bet we've got an interest in ways the game is won,
    far set the test is flowing before you're thriftily done
No chance at the sonnet, balanced best at ten; the
    ivy never covers how much it will pretend.
Until there in the last year, firmly set in class, the teacher
    claims, "No answers have I to help you pass."

Witch Hunt

Woe! Please tell me a story, a paragraph or two
the poem it only leaves me with a glime and time of you.
We once knew what we were thinking,
    and had no doubt at all.
Though now without a prose piece,
    we wander past our sphere
where words wink wildly wisdom and
    claim they will not come near.

Masters of Ceremonies

Drifts of cleverness, the wind forms on the
    field till the spring sings of foreverness,
    more than the world may yield.
Flowers fake their followers; the last truth they may stand
    once drama drops its actor upon the desert sand.
Free them from the fresh till all appears as stale, then
    most will they admire, the wicked winding tale.
Here now in this setting, where wishes weep and frost,
    a tear begins; its laughter at what the time has cost.
"Things were once so easy, not buried deep in doubt
    past points of recollection, on what it's all about."
I know, "Speaks up the withy; they're part of a tree,
    it's how we often want, more of others' poetry.
"Not quite," cites the shepherd, who knows
    best all his sheep. "My herd is hearing
    rhythms, no other flock may keep"
"Notes there for the feebleminded, if you
    wish to will. I'm more adhered to
    structure, see how it starts to fill."
"Whatever may you gather, for the sun sets low, the
    final entertainment begins the strongest show."

Vice and Folly

After we've played all our cards, the sun
  asleep behind the moon
where the words own all the bards, their
  crutch not sung in tune
There the end is hung on each moment
  through the forest we do walk
to hear the misspent mention having known
  once well how they should talk
Designs delivered by the starbeams, dancing
  through the wooded floor
tell us once this life is over, we'll still
  live to count the score,
Even though there will be none along for when we die
it's just another word wound 'round the perfect lie
If once the reason could stand clearly,
  without its fog and mist
we'd all know better when time may change the satirist

Misrepresented Societorical
Conditioning Cleansed

Law as is war, fundamentally up to one's spirit
  to decide, what is and what is not;
as well as when one is at and one is not at.

Not Habituated Or Ancient Lineage

1. MOMENTUAL., Relevant to a miracle play of the present
2. PATIUC, Unknown human ways, but to a few.
3. CINDRED, Less than the worth of ash.
4. HIMP, Taleteller and mind-taker.
5. CRISMIC, Poetic potential one notch above. Pronounced "cries-mick."
6. TWICH, Equivalent to twice laid, worthless wonderment-Skull Rot
7. NYCEKILLS, "Evening channels of pure water."
8. PAGAN, A large adjectival tag applied to a huge variety of spirit beseechers evolving in the 1980s.
9. POETEAK, A constructive or destructive written opinion upon a poem.
10. STRANGAHTEASE, Less describable emotional contacts, most often speckled with intellectual ties. Spelling is both singular and plural.
11. JESIENFUN, Enjoyment times ten.
12. POEFURORAWOSITY, Ones control of sound, pace, and word aim.
13. FOLLOWWING, Birdwatchers.
14. GUISEZITICALLY, Well-veiled and aloof thoughts of action.

A Taste Of Ketch

Send the sails, my salty crew, for bays
    may snort the likes of you,
The sky we'll sail above the sea, and shores
    for sure we'll have set free.
No wave on earth might mix our ship,
    as it pervades their inner grip,
On what to think or fancy, feel, only the
    poet knows what most is real.
They fake the locks on their mind, disclosing
    clearly what's far behind.

Jest Mind To Mind

All in fun, "I think not that
as juries stand and say they sat"
a judge, he lives a battered life
at best they're known for pain and strife
while pens and swords maze 'round their head
to mount the day when they're all dead.

Witch's Rite

In this land of page and word, only
    your thoughts are ever heard.
The two actors may swing and flow,
    reticently talk of what they know.
Where no loud shouts may catch the air, for
    minds to match or chance compare.
An ex cathedra pen and quest have written
    more than men may test.
Such pleasant times they dart the while to
    mark the heart of wisdoms' smile,
a daily treat we often take to want the
    words for winglet's sake.
The fool, he stares the jester down to
    see himself the only clown.
Well! Deeper goes the heart of mirth to
    give each word its very worth.
Where pranks dissolve to kindred sight and
    once decide what's wrong or rite.

Waves Of Wonder

Captain clever score your ship, 'fore one
    may sail 'neath your grip
our sights can see past nest of crows and
    figureheads sold first to rose
their visions vacant of wishful eyes, command
    the mind, its own surprise
till critics cry and wipe their tears away
    from all their deepest fears
each in tune and taught to note how
    much the poet once had wrote.

Highcouth

Beginning, middle, and an end, this is
  no novel, my reading friend.

Belcanto and Bellcrank

Bellcrank leaned a little to the left.
His skull had a distinct appearance.
Belcanto sang the band; he was adorable,
  though only to some.
They both had visions through their eyes
  as they evolved in a poem.
True characters, novel in style, romantic and
  rhyming till the hills boiled over.
They would chat on rare and only fair occasions,
  mostly about the words, ways, and smelly winds
  of others for whom they never cared much at
  all, if to begin or end with, nothing was ever
  well said nor nearly once well-written.

1. So much for the societorical dross 'neath every lifting eyelid. May
   their ashes achieve great rewards for no longer being part of this
   breathing mess.
2. Dim the salts, santa, think of them as sheep you no longer need to
   keep.

1. I suppose you're hooked on prose and all those punctuated flairs.
2. Never quite the chance for me, to write outside this world of poetry.
   It's in my mind and there to stay, come whatever or come what may.

1. That's good to hear and twice to read, I thought perhaps bitter notes
   inside your head as first I spoke and then had said, that 'neath every
   lifting eye is better off to sooner die.
2. Not the set of mind at all, I wish to see grow fat and tall. Select the
   few who step aside and take the unforgiving, ill-boding ride. Let
   their fashions coast amid the things most often wished we did.

1. Interesting set to say at least, these words that wind and start to feast on new ideas and styles to pose, 'fore many minds see what they've chose.

They both dissolve into a silent poem, having sensed
being overheard by the third eye.

Id And Ego Pending Over The Continuance

I wish the way we wage the will to make
    things move that all stand still.
"May not be done," demands the Don, while
    crumbled stage he stands upon.
"Still seems strong and real to me, both
    part of now and history."
Inside once might he strong look to find
    the meaning of each book.
Where dusted dawns and evenings air, set
    thoughts aside he can't compare.
New known nonsense claims his best, till
    dreams take on his neural test.

Belcantos Format

One studies his enemy or forever submits to defeat.

An Uneventful Reality for the Elite Media

We travel in disguise, through the spacious lives.
Deep in the seiche, sassy bark spins throughout
    the total pool, an abundant ordeal poison.
"Drink, read, drink," the silent mortician moans.
      "Sleep then think," my mistress postpones.
Spill the sea to drying streams, where dust
    still is seen inside our dreams.
No advise need be given, nor taken from its place
    that's sooner shown on one's own flumoxing face.

Re-Elected to the Inevitable

Unwanted.
On the dispersing end, dishing out an exit
    for the liquidated, solid, lord
word-cleansing wicked sword, slicing
    the lice upon our coats,
we dogs of wisdom cast then take all counted votes.

Unfamiliar with a Breathing Spell

One of shallow approaches, lost for words at a wink, trou-
bled by the times that cause one most to think.

One and Two

Why Stupe to Their Stupidity?

1. "No opposition, no gain."
2. "Arrogant aviator of the imagination, wind round your dead eyes. This sail must soon come down to ground."

1. "Dire you dangle thought before, with eyes that know not one of war. If simple was this life and death, I'd give you both to live without a breath. If hard was this old heart of mine, I'd stop its beat to pump its prime."
2. "You poetic nymph, cry to the moon for your yellowishness. Your blood has no color I have not seen, deeper goes all design than where you've ever been."

1. "No voyage may your sort ever set me upon, the sails of my life, all wage me as captain."
2. "Who made mention of the madding sea, first was it you, or first was it me?"

1. "My thoughts are now aboard all planes, and all ships. It's sooner to admit that I've lost all my grips."

The Obscure Outcome

Media manipulator controlling the unknown.
Till tomorrow at six, when it's unclearly shown.

At The Firing Range

An artist by accident, abstract at its best
A teacher in providence with no need to correct a test
A couplet crusader, a nomad to the crux
Constantly the invader whose head never ducks.

The Diverse City of Syndromes

Visually running through a thicket of symptoms,
    curing the causalities of seriousness.
Doctors demand their appointments; stillness
    and selectivity search the voice of free verse,
    dissolving the hinges of all doors.
The clock talks now; accomplished are,
    the endings of each moment.

The Eleventh Entrance

When handwriting falls by the wayside, and all keyboard
auto-printers see their demise, the word works worst of all
to open synthetic stupid eyes.

When You Think About It

The human mind's psychological potential often creates its own ceiling,
a roof of sorts, in constant need of replacing during the time of its dis-
and re-construction is when paraphrastic traits dissolve from character.

Disconstruction

Learning obstacles of the mind most often obtain this
action in order to develop one's own skilled experience.

Formulary Frontiers

Subject, size, and conversation,
Poetic ploys to seize the knees of the imagination.
Tricks and trumps with truer styles
See through these trees with stoic smiles

A Mona Lisa of the evergreen, no city
    sidewalks to dismiss her beauty.
She steps on each word her poet writes,
    portfolios of imagery pervade
Their reader's mind.
Till such songs are set and done, with fashion first,
'Fore notes are played nor nearly spun.

Owl Pass

An open mind is one that is into
    everything, both good and bad!
The poetic law we carve in stone, it sits alone.
Down the pike come Ike and Bill, leaders
    of the new political frill.

Lish

Pictorial ideas easily swithed by the mind.

Swithed

Brought beyond speed.

The Castaliancrave

Theoritician dyeing the verse
Inside the letters and art
Bring
Florries with storm and snow
Falling inside of the heart
Rhyming love's dreadful arrow
With feathers from the sparrow
Have fetters of meter drake
Shadowing our last mistake
Sop in wine beneath a poisoned tree
Growing close to shore to meet the sea

In the Olden Days of Dwindle Din

When little went right and all was thin
Feathered words did land on a silver page
And a gold lace sound spread across the stage
A crowd did draw to pass all the day
Till minds were happy with all they'd say

Fathominity = The ability to perceive beyond

The potentials of knowledge and wisdom

Seen Soon to Stagger

When thick grows the voice
The threads of this life
Wind round the spool of their choice
When down on ye luck
A rainbow will yield
Calling the clouds to lay low
Their blue and white shield.

Tonight We Will Drink

From the Pierian spring
Below the moon of wisdom
We will see everything
When they will dwindle
And cease before our feet
For never has man's mind
Had more it could meet.

The Moves of Wisdom

Near the weeping and worn
Have shadows that call
To the sun clearly born
Breaking the clouds that hover
This mysterious night
'Fore the last of wings find land
From the fathomless flight.

Contribute to the Literature

And crawl upon each line
The fleshly school of poetry
Has taught you how to thyme
The swords own shadow scares the weak
With little words they choose to speak
How bitter is thee way of pen
While still inside these plays of men
Each poet finds his way to bend.

Our Own Emblem

Knowable notes we all understood
Whether they're evil or crowning the good
They work at the opening next to the mind
Leaving the old cross far from our kind.

It's Well-Forgotten

Tones far under the porch and hall
Open their pitch and start to call
As the lightning strikes each chapter made
Until the memory forgets to fade.

Once Upon The Mat At Door

The key of the enclosure
Will let no one get out
Till the final frozen lock
Is thrown and tossed about
Tormented with red colors
Till they're taught to change
The Purpose of each ring that's worn
Appearing mighty strange.

Inscriptions for the Beings Phase

On the mountains chosen to raise
Lustrous influence lines each page
While hillsides steepen pioneers rage
A benevolent will has broken free
To take thee 'cross more written waves of sea.

David Gray's Gone to Dig Some More

Searching fame and poetic war
The Cornhill scripts have sold his view
As if before no one once knew.

In Stealth Schools of Criticism

Students drool and spit
The theme to every poet's dream
They cannot seem to fit
They read the titled, chaptered prose
And still decide that no one knows.

Scorn Through

All history has been clearly said
To grow the best inside a lady's head
Though warlocks know the cogent truth
That bites the best with wisdom's tooth.

Shaking Clear of Trammels

Unfinished on the easel
The treetops muse and stare
The wise and foolish wipe
The scenery from the air
Peasants seek the studio
For breadth of view and calm
'Til the spring is born and new
In a cloak it calls its charm.

Sense that Fails Still May Stand

To walk on by the closing hand
About to rule and take the knight
Down from his horse that's trained to bite
And the moment now and then
We find one man who moves the pen
He looks in darkness and has eyes
That see what never one's surmise
Battles on the moving key
Have been fought and won at sea
Though minds that melt and break like glass
Never have questions they may ask
Until they're formed to finely be
Away from all that is history
The absence in mind of creative thought.

Accomplished

When words run dry and voids appear
We fathom more what wizards fear
The stark and dark they shiver slight
As we perform this day and night
Below the skies and past their space
This poem has flown to now replace
What is thought to be and known as true
That's captured every part of you.

The Sun Yards Of Discription

The time for challenge has come
And the most descriptive plays
Acted on our marble stage
Are tombstones in each comer
That will decorate the page.

Hectivity = A fever created in the 1990s within the minds
of humanity for the need of nature.

Attilatic = A removal of all designs and foreshadowing of
ignorance appearing m the path of learning refinement.

Doff The Biblical Bribe

It's come to make you pay
Twelve men did walk to have us say
Attention to their plight
How right it must have been
Although we know the light
Was not all inside of them
Their lord has cursed the others
Whomever claims to be
Of the truer power
Or on top of sorcery
Now is not to curse a sin itself?
For he on mighty high
And who is known most often
For the reason men did die?

- The gleaning of certain new realities that arc inevitably with practice of sorcery.

Mirroritivity = Deep in reflective thought
Oiltprdnrer = A caster of the growing spell
Foliolcoptic = A poetic page of a sorcerer.

From Her Claws

Which lord will not ever know
What secret strings have been pulled
In this potioned puppet show.

Full And By deep

A harpoon in deep
Now part of the whale
With shrill voices that travel
From tongues toward the ear
Leaving in the memory
No skin to appear
They start begging a sailor
To slip on the deck
Where coins fall from the crow's nest
That flies from the wreck
Far over twigs on the wave
Near quills in the salt
The captain is blamed
And takes all the fault
The crew saunters off
Without any care
That their log is saved
And served to its share.

The Eye

What holds the tailor's tattered shreds
And printers broken type
As it has the apple fall
Before it's red or ripe
Then reads heroic verses
On throughout the naked night.

The Sac Tribe

Politics and politicians
Lose their value overnight
Though poets live forever
To teach us what is chiefly right.

Scop Doing That

Whoa! What a hatred the ink has in its pen,
It's been used upon half of all the earth's men.
"Not I," said the poet, "I am a romantic lover."
"Not 1," said the novelist, "it's scribed on the cover."
"Not I," said the playwright, "it's only been acted out."
"Then let there be no doubt, it's me," said the bad bard.
"Man has gone on for years,
And drown deep in his tears.
With all fears left about,
It's the coming of studious scholars
Who kill off the mellow, mild, and meek,
Planning to invade a world that is weak."

All Dogs Done Deliberating Over the Days Donations

The lasting cerebral wheels of want and space
Have starred the universe with each moon in place
Above the mountain's slope
Are shores of some who've sailed with hope
As on the hilltops of each man's wits
There ticks the time he most often quits
So supposed by those behind each door
Who'll not figure out any more.
The Universal Poet
Leaving on tramp ramp with bundle and stick
A travelling hedge smith thinning the thick
Fighting the griffon's hard bite and bark
Feeling it had found a man of no mark.

About the Way They See

Taking our towns for silver and beads
Filling our minds and gardens with weeds
Blind to the power of rain and sun
Knowing not where their spirit will run.

Wicked the Bantling

Who lives in these books
Compared to the schools
Of fish on their hooks
Easy the knowledge
Slips out through our hand
Holding the poetry
On its head so to stand.

The Lies You Wear

Tear and treat delight
Who wove them through this evening burning bright
Was it not the tongue of truth
That evades the scarlet letter?
Claiming all would see the day
When things had got much better
Or was it just the sounding cane?
Tapping near to where
You had placed your feet
As you did walk down Memory Land
With the poet who had lost his beat.

Prade=The art involved with the meaning of the word.

Props for the Clever

Candles and cloth
Deep in her spell
The witch watches her broth
Unknowing the masses
Will soon drink from its foam.
Then be off to the forest
To forever roam

About the Future

Words can twist a fate time to time
Still some grapes grow tart
While upon tile vine
The wicked marvel frequently
These days
For they can see clear through the bulky haze
Why the wisdom of
The most purest light
Has come to emanate
These words this night
Thus scapes the knowledge
To all baleful men
Unless they ask
The windward hand with pen.

Too Much Spice

A widow's curse of wicked words
Comes pouring out the ewer
Misunderstanding meets the night
From a long day on the shore
The tables set it will not fall
Its legs have most mighty knees
So place your order now!
Before the cook does what he please.

Flowlinatic= One who writes with excessive rhythm.
Foliofever = An obsession with reading or writing books.

Dealing With You

Wager down, good friend
Of the pursuit of knowledge
Ye have been overcome, think not what might
Bring the magic, for it has now begun.
To think the liquid serpents sail
Off to where no man s feet may run.
Or retell the clandestine tale
Which never claims that it is done.

A Perfect Landing

Two graving docks were once provided
For the tailor of vestries to land
Freeing the bridges from their toll
While snapping chains at his command
He stepped through the empty ash pits
To wipe the work clean from his hand
Once the answer had slowly rose
Above his footprints in the sand.

Footfalls on the Waterfalls

We know where each man fell
Though what of the great falls
That not a man can tell
Their secrets are our answer
And we never gave them doubt
Until we fathomed all
That said they were about.

No Belief in the Middle

Future present past
The seconds of the day
Are seen leaving fast
We want to hold them prey
Keep them from their end
Until we've found out how
Every one of them
Pretends about the now.

Midst the Livelihood of Peasants

Rough hewn their still feature spies
Finding friar books and sea drifts
Live inside of teachers lies
What's worth a few shillings
Will be sold as they meet
Not much for their spirit
And blistering of feet
Though a spark lights their twigs
Nigh by the foggy pond
That remakes with its flame
The lurking of each dawn
Where much less harsh a name
Is spoken out with scorn.

Spread Your Wings

Fly in the eye of the hurricane
Then fall on the stairs of defeat
Ye shall learn of the winds and their wrath
Leaving a taste not mentioned as sweet
Which turns on the wings of the falcon
Then glides on the strength of the breeze
To land in the nest of knowing
Where spirits hide the field from the trees.

From A Stolen Reality

Closing the lid
Of the public's proud eye
Thieves take to the night
Toward the gold nearby
As chance would have it
They make off and guzzle away
Before deacons discover
Their gifts are gone far astray.

Fathom the Mischievous Folklore

A teaser at times with a tune that will twist
Like a hand through the fog all covered with mist
A design of a dream drawn from our sleep
Inside of the secret dear Clotho will keep
Side of the fire where the willows weep flame
Is coming a voice which gives each verse its name.

Knot the Slight Tease

Dropping from the roofs of the minds
The barrel will fill to soon over spill
Moisture for the grape on the vines
That are crushed to ply without the dregs
Keeping them safe in wooden kegs.

Inside Everything

Peer through the odd oracles
That this evening has found
And what they will tell about
As they slowly come around
Sails in a full wind, a breeze in the air
Times and their talents, hidden will not share
Why has the captain fallen from the stem
Without a care of floating
On the sea that has us learn?

Remove The Dust From Bookends

Remarkable personages of the times
March on the depths of thought
Regarding what rhymes
And has had their attention caught
From old walls and towers they look
But cannot be simply freed
For the barghest and the bard
Have planted their every seed.

The Mirror Kills

To See The Mirror Kills

Maudlin madness, mixed into each myth
We will read through their stories
Completing the fifth
The pawns they sit lonely though with the sun
Our reflection has started to say we've begun.

To Evelyn

Whose presence always brings me closer
To lovely heavens place
Where forever I will not forget
The beauty of her face
So many times she has made real
This life we live on earth
That I know now that none compare
To all that she is worth.

I Love Her

Eve may hold no candle to her
Nor the purpose of her design
Love may not describe the beauty
She brings each day inside my mind
Words they will wander weak
Though these I pray will find her eye
Then softly start to speak
And tell all the reasons why.

Let Me Count The Reasons

Tactful, humble lady
A pearl that has no price
Kind and considerate
Beyond the point of nice
The fairest of Lord's creatures
Features rarest and most fine
I treasure all her presence
Beyond every point in time.

Washed Up

The ship is going under, its sails are on the wave
The parrot speaks to sailors now nearing more their grave
"Now my perch is sinking, and the tight door to my cage
For you fools have not learned of the sea and all its rage
You've fed me and kept me behind cold, rusted old bars
Although never will you know the secret words of stars
Deep may your souls sink, then wash
    to the abandoned shore
Where landlubbers will laugh at your salty rotten core."

Shore You Understand

The proud parrot flies to shore to
    find one sailor still alive
He lands upon his shoulder to ponder
    why he did survive.
"You once did clean my cage and took
    me walking on the deck
Past the plank where others had left
    this life to last inspect
How quickly thoughts had flown beyond
    bright lights and battered times.
And are you not the sailor who first
    brought the crew to rhymes?"

Two The Best

"Aye! my dear bird
I'm the one who sailed each poetic wave
Though still, deeper do I wonder
Why you, the sea did save.
Did you not drop on my wooden leg
With threat to ply your beak inside my keg?
For me you may never fathom
Though most well I know your wings
And now I'll teach you wicked verse
That forever sticks and stings."

Naughty Nautical Tars Aboard

Gunwales and scaly fish stares on crew
Tired of harpoons and nets they once threw
So well-entangled in their buccaneer dream
Well-sailed and thought to be a piratic team
Far beyond the flicker and the sound
Of the foghorn's blow
Planning the plunder of galleys
When seen sliding slow.

The Pirate's Point

Sorrow on their lowered sails
From the other's telling tales.
How they've learned to take a wave
And sail on to their hell.
With stories sunken deeply
Beyond the time to tell.

H.A. Poetry

They once called it clever
Though they know not what to say
For we have taken words
They wish that they could say.

Tow Row

Scarce the songs that last through the years
Many the eyes that fill with tears
Watching close as their ship sinks low
Into the depths where they must go
To find what must become of golden rhymes
That tell much more of earth than troubled times.

I am Not So Sure

The shore has felt each keel and leg
That walks below a weaving dreg
No one knows better count on bow
That he wills not to speak right now.

Bee Cause

Bees see the people coming toward their hive
Curiously they wonder
Without wings and stingers, how they'll survive
"If not for our sweet honey and the beauty of our queen
Never would we be on this earth or seen."

Swallow The Wind

Whistle words to near a taste
Which weave their meaning on in haste
The world would say it's been their way
As it spins its web both night and day.

Scops Doing It

How old the way that nature knows?
To spring and fall toward blowing snows.
As poets make this earth to ring
With verse and word of future thing.

Above Our Hull

Gray dust of death on hangman's breath
Has blown beneath the stone
Where corpse and bone
With hollow skull
Rests themselves alone.

OH Crossbones

Blown in the back by blood's wildest storm
They stood on deck to first be born
United on the plank nearby
The sword tip decides now who must die.

They Watch The Warning Pattern

When night life stops and draws a blank
Then refuses not to ever thank
Advice and answers without a score
Rowing free through its open door.

Abitas

Shells of abalone we'll see
Before the tide has counted three
The lines are cast to catch their bait
As beaches meet each foe of fate.

Sailing Courage In The Heart

Paint in fresco, find the lines
As ropes on anchors used at times
Beneath the bay the water still
Treasure chest with written will
Be out of verse to spit and curse and walk on warbled deck
In storms of lies that read below
How close they might inspect
The net that's worn with salty dive
Has lost a meal or two
As weathered eyes look out to sea
And sail the night on through to be.

Set Fast

Back to the seapins the cushion is bare
No words of the voyage on lips did they dare
Secret the sound the rhyme in the light
Told to old sailors on shipboard at night
A net is the best we'll challenge the hook
To catch all the notes in log for our book
Silver is grade and coins have their purse
As pirates have made each sail for the worse.

All The Power Of Knowing

Load your guns and raise your swords
Though thy pen has more might
Than your artificial lords
It writes through the bitter cold
Bringing rays of warm sunshine
Upon eyes and hands that hold
To the metered mellow mire
Where minds sit complete and free
Watching verses catch on fire
Pound your fist as poets do
This rhyme has not run clearly through
Stomp your feet as soldiers may
For never will it give a way.

Ring

If flowers grew without a stem
I would say that is fine
Though really all they've done
Is grown upon a vine
If people talked without a tongue
I would say that is great
Though really all they've said
Is I can now relate
If nighttime had the light of day
And daytime had the dark
The world would be another place
And life another start
Miracles are just a thing
Which make us not feel blue
And this poem, a small deed
That you may once see through
Call it light and not so deep
Without a word profound
Until you read it once again
And like it for its sound.

Into The Poetry Of Spirit

When life will last forever
And nothing ever dies
Reason will raise its hand
And slowly wipe its eyes
Of tears and dust that collect
Behind the world and sun
Where life once quickly passed
A part of everyone.

Put To The Sword

A fancy for a sea-faring wildlife
Quenched by pirates and the curve of their knife
Then back to their old silent shore
Where no winds take the mind off to explore
The bold waves rising below the rough and unkind
Now on the plank being bound and blind.

Bouquets of Solomon's seal

Wiltin' 'bout the castle with its loss of appeal ever
    since the witch of the wondrous wood
Has moved within its walls to spread
    her spells of no good.
Her garment is black 'neath her silver-lined cape
And her curse is well-known to all that
    they may never escape.
What wrong had they done to deserve this hard fate
To lie restless at night and be clothed by her hate.
Might there be no mercy that would allow them to sleep?
And their dreams of before will she always keep?
Now rest will come to this land
If they all at once read this poem and start to understand.

Bearing Them Harmless

Twier with greetings, carpets rolled out
Into the voids of dire doom and doubt
As spring rain takes the thirst from the driest of palm
Holding the earth from its day of calm.

In The Sittish Pendraughtsman

The low light lines of the letter press have
        their times they unruly confess
to flagrant tales 'bout the freelancing floss while
        out to sea where their meaning is lost
they'll stand on the shore as they melt 'way the frost
on the listening minds that are terribly tossed.

Style Weighted With Matter

In olden days of dwindle din
When little went right and all was thin
Feathered words did land on a silver page
And a gold lace sound spread 'cross the stage
A crowd did draw and paint 'way the day
'Til minds were happy with all that they'd say.

Those Pixilated Fools

Trying to sink us then take our treasure home
Even though we know they're bound to waves that roam
The seas and mighty plenty more
They cannot have our verse or core.

Historically Firist

Inscriptions for the being's phase
On the mountains chosen to raise
Lustrous influence lines each page
While hillsides steepen pioneers rage
A benevolent will has broken free
To take thee 'cross more written waves of sea

The Wizard Of Wameful

Those who've dealt with us unjust will die
by the tip of the quill
the blade of the sword
'neath the feet of their unfit lord.

CONTEXTUAL = All fitting in theory.
DIEPIACENT SPELLS = The removal
    of unnecessary life forms.
GLEANATIVE LEVEL = Where there
    is an uncontrollable series of ideas
    resulting in human brilliance.
IPLANTATION = One's prospects for the future.
PHOTOGLIMPSISTIC = One who is able to arrange
    art forms with coinciding word arrangements.
PLYTWISTARIAN = An artistry that changes the
    understanding of all life itself repeatedly.
SORCEROUS LIBRATORY SKILL = Diligently
    devised diction that plays the largest part
    in the evolution of mankind's mind.

"Surreptitious Spells are created by thoughts with certain
words that trigger the magical elevation of consciousness."

A Wolf hit page, ABOVO.

Cursing Inwardly

"Woe! My mind has blistered," whined
  the wicked old king,
"These coins from the peasants do
  not mean a damn thing.
This red robe from my tailor hangs like an old rag
As bells in the tower tell how long the days drag.
This kingdom has crumbled, and I need none of its sort.
Its soldiers are dusty as though never they have fought.
Romance has been hiding back the morning's odd moon.
And my minstrels know nothing of the pleasure of tune.
My queen, she has wintered and twists slowly in her bed
From the dreams that I've placed in
  the cellars off her head."

She's So Beautiful

I've been chosen the maid to clean this nasty wolfs den
Where bats fly from the words I'd sooner meter to ten.
To the strong head of the pack that
  once surely slept in this cave
Then woke to scavenge the earth of
  what it could no longer save.
This lair has me linger and wonder
  long how they had thought
For I might once compare myself to their restorative lot.

To Gather In the Brotherhood

Beneath my crude cape and veil
Inside this mind runs a tale
Written for thy lie buries itself so long and dreadfully deep
To rise in the spirit no others keep.
The true tongues they hang all day in bells
As the cobbler knows more the sole that often tells
Which way the path to put things right?
Though never does it come in sight
Still we do have this chilly poem
To walk us down our road alone
Let's take this page and see its clear pure flame
To design more perfect our written game.

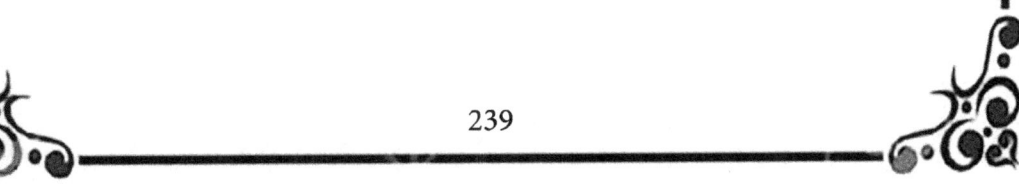

The Meaning Of The World

Who alive holds the boldest pen on earth,
and where might its feathers have had their birth?
Are they mad and mean?
Or more mostly nice?
Do they gamble at night and roll the dice?
Or just make bets inside this deck of cards?
As we have read through these old cold graveyards.
These stones they hold the words so neatly bold
may be believe all that we are now told.
It reads so real that sure this one has gone
"yond the faith our minds might not carry on.
"Well, let's stop and face it;
in the first degree of stupidity we sentence thee."
"Woe, such a hard, merciless, and ruthless plan.
How is it that you've seen I could not understand?
All this wide world and its most mighty match,
perhaps in myself I'll more further catch."

What The Nest Had To Say About It

The difference from a memory and thought
Are very little if you have never caught
That the moment now comes at this time
And before was built much more for a rhyme
The sense you make and feel most right
Though it soon disappears from sight
For the gears of the mind are best known
To the poet who has clearly shown
How rare the man who more often thinks
Inside his head where the mind's eye winks
Then passes back behind the last of light
That would shine bright upon his quill in flight.

Us

These books we read jest at the start
Their beat and blood it knows the heart
Some have followed their mighty lord
Thinking they had once come aboard
Others took the path more further south
And left the words inside their mouth
Then too many found their own perfect way
To show this world what they could say
We are the ha-ha's and may laugh all night
At others that wish we'd die 'side their spite
Today within this verse and poem
Our sympathy goes out to those who've
thought that they have known.

Everything

Slings and arrows fly by my head
While others lie there rotting dead
Mess their mind, I would indeed
Though it's not worth thy time nor speed
Who takes them from this world so fast?
For sure their nothingness will never last
He's come on here with many names
And even she has made her mighty claims
If it's not most clear by now
Who has the power to show us how
'Twill never be nor once come true
That only one has seen completely through.

Inside Their Wives Ears

Ah! Vast varieties of visions vying for their victory tall
Mighty misty moments ticking upon the wall
Tearing the English to simple little shreds
Sitting poetic so neatly within their heads
Just outside thy high heavenized hell
We shall listen to the romantic rumors that
the wizards wish they could tell.

With Hands On Their Throats

When mystery leaves and all peers clear
Then men admit how much they do fear
The sounds of selves seeking out
The vanished bits of bitter doubt
The tailor thinks of seams sewn wrong
And prays the minstrel plays his song
'Stead of waiting on the night
To have its clouds and poets
Set the yellow moon more right
As the sailor wants the wind to be
His closest friend when far out to sea
The generals want the victory
To quite quickly claim their secret name
Though the jester tells them all this time
The joke shall not ever clearly thyme
Nor repeat quite the same in mime.

Digesting Silence

Travelling trouble on a tombstone tide
Has flown with the feather and spear by side
Hunting the white man where he'll always hide
Deep in the forest or lost in the field
The knights no longer have their solid shield
To stop the arrows of tragical truth
It tastes each lie with blood and pointed tooth.

Beginning To Work On It

In soups of stupidity
Boils the empty, endless dine
One may say that we have begged
For eyes knowing sun will shine
Call the classes to their rooms
That they might sleep and see no more
Of the wizard and his will
That sets this earth to constant chore.

In Just A Matter Of Rime

Who's clever enough to climb every line
That has been cast out by sailors writing this rhyme?
Who's sly enough to have seen the knot near the top
Where no one's imagination may ever stop?
Suppose it was Plato in some theory thought through?
Or by now have ye solved that it's suddenly you
Taking the eye and deer of the wood
Thinking that they only should, if they could
Count the rare moments that most
    matter mixing with mirth
Shrouding this mysterious world that calls itself earth.

Thyself Thinking, More Than Ever

Behind the wide wall works our wonder with whips
Though slowly our fine mind suddenly slips
Into the pit where we will meet Mr. Poe
Who knows more than any president could know
Say nothing of Dickens, he's a dire, doomy bird
Who writes beyond masters these states every heard
Now who holds the flame, that burns
    most sure inside the mind?
look onward, my dear readers, and forever you'll find.

Of The Poetry

When will the ego more soon disappear
That no longer it causes our minds to have fear
When will the quill fly far off on its own
To give us the verses no others have yet known
When will the wild wizard wind our wishes most right?
That no others may keep us in their sight
We fast sight a beggar at the bottom of the lot
For we've looked more hard and sure
Than once any have thought.

Have You Any Eye Dear

My how they fall on the sidewalk so small
For they may soon yell or start their slow crawl
Toward the bell in the tower that tells surely each hour
Ticking right on toward thunder and
    the sound of our power.

A Mirror Cause

Sew, and the plot thickens
'Til you have finished with Dickens, Poe, and all the others
Thy must know the finest brothers
We've told you to see and suddenly be
　　part of the truest poetry
Now that our chips have been taken and
　　more than gravely mistaken
Your eyes finally awaken
To their last thoughts being shaken
To the furthest of silent shores
Where no false Columbus explores.

Tedesco Taube

On a nodule of earth beggars come near
Hoping that these words will bring them no fear
Weak and listless, limbering souls
Up to the altar where only one knows
How to prepare best their little weak mind
Into depths where no one may find
Who has come down upon this fine round earth
And given these poems much more to be worth.

From Your Own Stew Pit Did Tease

These deep amounts of wit never seem to fit
Not even the slightest bit
How might all soon admit
This world has turned to sit
Inside its own, you know verse
That causes all to curse
Upon thy sheltered wheel
That your mind might once reveal
How much it has to steal.

Wonder

If I were to write your mind underneath
And all that you've known in constant belief
Would you try to sink the thoughts that I may think?
If I were the man that turns this whole world 'round
Would you think that you had suddenly found
The ideas of wizards welcoming Rome
To be falling again inside your own?

The Great Spirit Bows

Dew knots itself to the field
The sun will rise 'side each yield
I've taken more than any might give
And gone far beyond all that may live
Flown higher than any with wines
And known more than many of things
Disgraced the highest of power
Bloomed and fallen from each flower
While telling the most pleasant of springs
What will go on inside of all things?

Noah, What I am Talking About

Might I write your own wonder
So wicked and wild that it woes
Beside my wary widows
Where Wishful willows take blows
With breezes of the English
An island unknown to man
So powerful the Bible
Has to make itself understand

Inside Immortal Complexities

How many pages an eye has to read
'Fore it has realized its life passed with speed
Tangle with truth, then unraveled with a little white lie
Remember the poetry never lives, nor does it die.

With Poetic Inspiration

Take a loan out on insight, then call yourself real
Though thy purse is greatly worn and has holes
Only those looking downward may ever once steal
Away with our faults and greatest of need
'Til verses decide whom they may first feed.

With The Old Switch-A-Roo

Herbs they have taken these times we call ours
Spreading good health and the strangest of powers
The hungry they always seem to appear
Climbing the wall built from hunger and fear
We sit there fat or thin as a vine
Though never they know how quickly we rhyme.

Of Their Power

There are witches who bite and bring on the storm
There are ones who will love you at night
    and say nothing is wrong
Some they might tell you of a wizard with pen
Writing inside the lives of all men
Some they may cast the most beautiful spell
Telling you never to say, nor to tell.

Now Everything

There is a prince
who walks through each long day
There is a king and czar
with queens close to play
There is a blind butcher
with the most finest cut of meat
There is also a tailor
who's turned each seam into pleat
Though why does the wizard
work so hard at not being seen?
Might the reason come near
if we were not so quick to dream?

Our Minds Are Set Better To Thought

Little wild looks glance from the corners of eyes
Gifts waiting well-wrapped
Know themselves the surprise
Fields full of wheat
Sight hot ovens far off with loaves of bread
As poets plan more to improve the next things to be said.

Theurgic Thinkers

By now we have noticed these lines weave a net
Around we foolish fish that feel we may bet
Our odds are the highest and stand nearest to our play
Though we know more will be gleaned
in the way that we say.

The Questions Its' Own Answer

Secrets are not kept inside one's own fingers or big toe.
Love never forms in the heart, though
    they think they know.
All it has plan and comes only from the purest mind.
And there never has been anything else one may find.
Still they may murmur and say with their heart
They love this world and know how it did start.
Fools, they are many and grow more numerous each day
'Til the hand of death sweeps them up and out of the way.
To have spirit is not only inside of what lives,
'Cause death lasts much longer and also more often gives.

Where We Started

We're wild dregs and fine dancers no
    rune knows not our ears
Of World War II, we are veterans that live with few fears.
A bomber is our best friend, and may
    the dams blast and bust
It is a cold day in hell when our fury will rust.

How To Be The Captain

How have they come to this bold ferry so small?
Wishing the other side where sooner they'd crawl?
Has the beauty of water enticed their narrow view?
Or is it something forever they wish they once knew?

Yale You're Stupid

May the better grow bleaker from the sights we have seen
Might they become weaker with sleep in our dream
"Damn!" the king pounds his fist on the floor
"Why have not these wise poets come forth to my door?
I'm the czar and sweet president for
    four years I've been such
How is it that I've been so far out of touch?"

Basilisk The Creatress, She's So Beautiful

Of course! Times they fly the highest mission
To wish they had a passage on the sea
Others look through windows
Wishing they may once see the you or me
Their eyes with sleepers, tears, then pupils proud
Forever search among the lost and distant crowd
They're folks who have a glass they wish
    never would fall or break
Though as a child there were fragile pieces
    we all wanted to make or take
Still perhaps the women are the weakest
    and have won far too many wars
Although forever will most men not escape
    their sharp, poignant claws.

Everything Born Again

Chimneys line the roofs
and smoke it knows their place
Set high above the heads
that all know a wrinkle on their face
What of the doors that will not open and
    stand frozen in their case
Still more we may quondamly know
If our memory would once erase.

Upon The Seven Slaves Of Stupidity

Far from the scraps of our minds desire
Ride the weak enemies in fast pursuit
Of what they shall not withstanding know
Nor never make a proper swift salute
The women and the delicate children.
Woe! Yes, first they must leave each sinking ship
To not understand the will's strong courage
Of the captain that cracks the final whip.

With Chief

Might the wonders of a woman come
    down upon you and never leave
Through the powers of a man are none
    that any may once perceive
May the ocean flow beyond all shores that could enhance
How the natives of this country have
    taught the world to dance.

To Get Interesting

Inside the rumble, tumble weeds
As the imagination starves, it feeds
The hungry, hiding horrors of the night
That live and give quills that write
Away our worst and wanting, wilting sins
There with breath this life begins.

Feeling Born Again

The most precise purchase of all our understanding
Is when the hammer hits profoundly the head of nail
Pure and peerless the legend rises
From the lines well-written in the tale
Rhymes surround this universe
And leave it lost with no sleep
Unless you count the moments
Inside minds that wish to keep
Probing the parish among its little rows and pews
That never seem to fathom the best of all good news.

Bout Us

Mull and mingle in the voids of nothingness
Such as so much of mankind has had its will
Like lords and gods before us
That said forgive the sin to kill
These cheeks they grow with reddish roses
And prey upon those who quickly turn
To forget for any slight moment
How much they have to learn.

You'll Always Need Protection

Yes, I'm the wild wizard, designer of each golden throne
That lets wicked and wild, both men and women sit alone
I have more aides than any earth could ever have known
And I'll make Hitler look like he never could have shown

About the Author

Born in Great Falls, Montana, Fletcher De Wolf was raised mostly in Alexandria, New Hampshire.

Fletcher appreciates the wonders of nature and the wooded beauty of New England. Employed as a social worker, the author finds time to compose music, play the guitar, do woodworking, and write a great deal of good poetry.